GRIT, GUTS, AND C4

The Sapper School Experience

Ryan Andrew Voznick

Preface

MAY 31–JUNE 27, 2008

I did not write this book for an audience. I wrote it so that I would never forget the events that occurred during my time in Sapper school and can relive them if I so choose. It would be extremely difficult for me to forget the events described herein, but memory, even mine, grows dusty over time. The following is my attempt—and a feeble one at that—to describe my experiences up to, during, and after attending the US Army Sapper Leader Course at Fort Leonard Wood, Missouri. Before I begin, I would like to mention that I have changed the names of the ROTC and Sapper instructors as well as two of my classmates. Finally, when it comes to any type of training in the military, individual experiences may vary. This account is as honest as I could make it, but I know that those who have gone before and since may have a different interpretation. There are many factors that contribute to this, including age, previous military experiences, and level of physical conditioning. I want to emphasize that this is *my* personal experience.

CHAPTER ONE
Preparation

"You better get that tab, Voznick."

In early February 2008, Captain (CPT) Jones, a member of the Reserve Officers' Training Corps (ROTC) cadre at San Diego State University, sent an e-mail to all completion cadets. (Completion cadets are those who finish the program by the end of the school year but do not commission until the year after.) The e-mail stated that the program had received an application for a slot to Sapper school and that one lucky individual would get a shot at attending the "third toughest" school in the army. Completion cadets were the only ones eligible in our class, which left only three candidates: Cadet (CDT) Jappe, CDT Todd, and myself.

Apparently, I beat both of them to the ROTC office and spoke face-to-face with CPT Jones. I let him know I was interested, and he printed out the Sapper Leader Course (SLC) information pamphlet for me from the Sapper website. I knew very little about the school, even after reading the course information from the SLC website. In addition, nobody had been to Sapper school in our ROTC battalion. I also needed an Army Physical Fitness Test (APFT) score of 290 or better and was a bit disappointed because my most recent scores were only in the 260s and 270s—not my standard. I had slacked off due to the demands of being a senior and working for ROTC.

CPT Jones told me to inform Todd and Jappe of the opportunity and ask if they were interested in the school. I called them both soon after, and of course they were both very interested. I figured that one of them would get the slot because both had better PT scores, but I was persistent. For the next few days, I dropped by the office just to see if anything new had developed in the cadre's decision about who would go. The "turn in" date for the application came quickly, and I happened to be in the office when they made the snap decision: send Voznick.

I filled out the paperwork, which included an essay on why I should be selected for Sapper school. When it came to the PT score and the mandatory 290, I assured CPT Jones that I could get a 290 by the next PT test. He went to bat for me on that one (on the application he put 291 as my current score and apparently wrote some very nice things about me), and it took a few weeks to get the reply back from Cadet Command. The answer I received from Cadet Command concerning whether I would go or not was, in hindsight, probably the worst answer I could have gotten.

Apparently, Cadet Command wanted to fill twenty slots. It had selected sixteen cadets to go to the school and four alternates to back them up. (An alternate is an individual who replaces a cadet if he or she becomes sick or injured and thus is not able to attend the school.) I was the fourth alternate. Lieutenant Colonel (LTC) Smith, the battalion commander, personally called me and let me know. He conceded that I was probably not going to be able to attend the school, and that I should focus on my grades and ROTC instead. My response to this was a simple shrug of the shoulders. For the rest of the semester, I focused on ROTC and my grades, scoring a 4.0 grade point average for the first time ever. I also, therefore, didn't work very hard to improve my PT score. CPT Jones warned me that I should be wary because Sapper school "could still happen" for me. In the back of my mind, I was a bit concerned, but I carried on as I had been doing, regardless.

I got a surprise on the first day of May. Major (MAJ) Sanchez, another member of the ROTC cadre, called me and asked if I could be ready to leave May 9 for Sapper school. I was shocked, but the answer to this question was easy for me. In my mind the reply was absolutely and unequivocally "no." I was about to enter finals week, and my grades were still necessary for my accessions, the time at which the ROTC would evaluate me for my duty in the army.

This would be my last chance to raise my GPA, and I was willing to sacrifice anything to make it happen. The major said he understood and let Cadet Command know that I was not available for May 9.

The repercussions of that decision were not surprising. All of my peers who didn't understand my decision, and even some of those who did, gave me dumbfounded looks. "Did you really give up a slot at Sapper school?" they asked incredulously.

"You're damn right, I did," I replied. "It's finals week; are you crazy?"

Of course, they did not understand this. Most of the ROTC cadets were conditioned to sacrifice grades for army training, so I had anticipated their reactions. In fact, they poked fun at what appeared to be a cop out. Some of them kidded that I had bailed on a one-time opportunity and that I was "weak sauce." I didn't care what they thought because I knew I was making the right choice, but about a week later, I called home.

I had already made detailed plans for how I was going to spend my summer, but when I called my mom a few nights later, I said, "There is a chance that I will get called up for that Sapper school I talked about a few months ago. I was an alternate and not supposed to go, but they tried to get me to go on the ninth." After coordinating some dates with Mom, I hung up and went to bed for the night.

The next morning, I awoke to the sound of my cell phone ringing. I had forgotten to turn down the volume, and I was pissed off when I saw that the number was from ROTC. "The bastards never stop being a pain in the ass," I thought. I ignored the call and rolled back over. Two minutes later, it rang again—another ROTC number—and then I knew exactly what was happening. Even before I answered, I knew that I was going to Sapper school. It was CPT Jones, and he was excited when he asked me if I could be ready to leave May 27. I was hesitant. The truth was that I had been working out in preparation for the school, but I figured I was not doing anywhere near the amount I needed to be truly ready for it (I was not).

I mumbled a response because I had just woken up. CPT Jones told me to call back in half an hour after I had "cleaned out the cobwebs," and give him a straight answer. I got out of bed, took a shower, and called my parents. I ran the dates past them, and then I called CPT Jones and gave him the OK. It all happened in less than an hour. Now I was in it for sure, and I knew I had quite a bit of work to do before leaving. I just didn't know what work that was.

Knowledge is power. That is a favorite saying of mine. So in order to prepare for Sapper school, I wanted to know everything I could about the training. I began asking the cadre detailed questions about the course, but instead of getting help or concrete advice, I received replies like, "You better get that tab, Voznick," and "You're going to be tabbed as a cadet, Voznick. That's badass!" The Sapper "tab" is a small six letter patch that is affixed to the left shoulder upon successful completion of the school. There are only four "tabs" authorized in the Army.

None of this made me feel very comfortable or more prepared, and I continued to seek help. The cadre misinterpreted my questions as a lack of confidence and a desire to "cop out." I was somewhat impressionable, and when CPT Parson told me, "Voznick, it's an army school. It's going to suck, but it's set up for you to pass," I felt a bit more at ease. Indeed, I wasn't doing terribly. I scored a 290 on the last PT test of the semester, and got a phone number from CPT Jones of someone who had previously attended Sapper school.

I called the Sapper school graduate, and when I asked him about the rest cycle at Sapper school, I mentioned that the Sapper school paperwork states the working day ends at 2200 and starts at 0500. I also mentioned that I had heard that during the field training, we are only allowed four hours of sleep per night, and I wanted to know if that were true. There was a long, quiet pause over the phone, and then he replied, "Honestly, four hours of sleep is more than you'll ever get, especially in the field." I was somewhat dismissive of this information. After all, it was in the course description that the working day ended at 2200! I wouldn't find out how accurate his words were until I was at the school.

All things considered, I still didn't feel as if I was adequately prepared. I had more than enough help training up, and I had plenty of time to prepare for airborne school and the Leadership Development Assessment Course (LDAC). However, I felt I was going at this "Sapper school" entirely alone and with very little preparation time.

I had two weeks from the time I received the phone call to the day I was supposed to report to Fort Leonard Wood to prepare myself. Finals week and the ROTC commissioning ceremony took away one of those weeks, so I had to make do. (I was made the sound tech for the commissioning ceremony. I felt that nobody in ROTC seemed to be taking my attendance at Sapper school very seriously.) I spent the last week trying to fill out the Sapper school packing list, which caused me much aggravation and a personal loss of over $400. The cadre didn't ask me how I was doing, or if I needed any help. They didn't ask me anything concerning my preparation, or provide any real guidance. I footed the bill and received my orders the day before I left for Chino, my hometown.

The day finally came, and my dad drove me to the airport. "You don't want to go, do you?" he stated. He had been keeping up with my situation and trying his best to help me out where he could.

I tried to stay optimistic. "Nah, I'm ready. I just wish they had told me a bit earlier and I had been a little more prepared, but I'll get by." I felt the folks in San Diego were being unsupportive, but there is another saying I like: "Real courage is starting out knowing you're licked, and saddling up anyway." Winston Churchill said that one, and I felt (and in the next few weeks repeatedly felt) that this statement applied to me especially.

The plane ride out was interesting. A thunderstorm shut down the airport in Texas, and I was a day late to Missouri. In addition, the prop plane that flew me into Fort Leonard Wood hit a bird right outside my window just before landing. Black feathers went everywhere. One of the props was shattered, but we landed no worse for wear. I was in Missouri with plenty of time before "zero day" of the Sapper Leader Course.

I arrived with a few days to spare before training began. I met with the other cadets and practiced my knots. Somehow, they had prior knowledge of the knots, and most of the cadets had the knots memorized before arriving. They said their schools had hooked them up with all the information. Apparently, mine was the only one that did not forward me the knots information, which was on par for San Diego State University Army ROTC. Therefore, I immediately began practicing the knots.

I did not care too much for these cadets. It seemed that they were all "army happy" or, as Mike Jappe phrased it, they were "army nerds and geeks." They were clean-cut and acted like police officers who had just pulled someone over. I knew that I would get along better with the regular army guys when they arrived. When they did, it was the night before "zero day," so there was not much time to get to know everyone in the barracks.

"Zero day" was uneventful and involved only in-processing and a standard precombat inspection (PCI), an inspection to ensure that each trainee had brought the required gear. Actually, I almost lost my chance to attend the school at this point. My DODMERB, or army physical form, was expired, but by sheer luck, the medic didn't notice and allowed me to pass. Why my ROTC allowed me to attend the school without an updated medical form was beyond me, but at that point, I didn't care (again, this kind of stuff was on par for my school).

Day one was also relatively uneventful. We received a course overview and conducted our PT tests in the morning. I scored a terrible 255. The grader had been tough on my push-up form for some reason, and my run was below average. I don't think I was well acclimated to the weather, but it didn't really matter. As long as I received a passing grade, my training was assured.

In the afternoon, however, we began our first real training and got a small taste of things to come. We took a medical class and learned how to start an intravenous (IV) line on someone. This is where the training started to worry me a bit. We were *talked* through how to insert the needle and use the other equipment of the IV, and then we were told to be ready to execute the entire procedure at "combat speed" on a live patient right after the twelve-mile foot march on day three. *Are you fucking serious?* I thought. I hate needles, and the thought of actually having to *give* someone an injection with no prior experience didn't make me feel too well. I didn't know it then, but this "shotgun blast"-type of instruction was the cornerstone of Sapper school training. I never really got used to it, but we all adapted to it and carried on as best we could.

To cap off the evening, we had a level one combative class and were released early (I think about 1900). On my way back to the barracks, my evaluation of the whole course was "so far, so good." There were no sergeants screaming at the top of their lungs and no absurd timelines, just good army training. We were here to learn a skill, and the instructors were going to provide us with the tools to succeed. In about twelve hours, though, that analysis would be proven terribly wrong. What was coming the next morning would be the first of several experiences that kicked me in the nuts at Sapper school.

CHAPTER TWO

Down to Business

"This place is…crazy."

I awoke in the morning and, despite the tenseness that permeated the air, calmly dressed myself in my PT gear. Before departing the barracks, I cut a piece of parachute cord and tied a chemical light around my neck as ordered by the Sapper instructors the night before. Today was our first graded PT session. If we failed to conduct a task to Sapper standards, my chemical light would be broken and I would not receive any points. I was still very complacent and confident that I would have no problems on the three-mile run scheduled for that morning.

I did not have an easy time keeping up with the seven-minute-mile pace combined with the warmth and humidity associated with the southernmost areas of the Midwest, but I managed it somehow. Upon completion of the run, the exhausted finishers circled up. (About a third of the initial class of forty-five was still with us; the rest had fallen out.) We had been running for over twenty minutes. At this point when we were in ROTC, we would have stretched out and dismissed the formation. After an all-too-brief cooldown, the Sapper instructors (SIs) ordered us into a PT formation. The first exercise was side straddle hops (jumping jacks). We ended up doing 200 four-count side straddle hops before switching to another exercise.

I noticed that the SIs had no qualms about breaking chemical lights. The cracks were audible over the cadence, and I realized that there were about four

SIs patrolling our ranks, ensuring that we were doing the exercises correctly. The slightest infraction resulted in a broken chem light. We did exercises for what ended up being a full hour (not including the run). Each exercise was designed to destroy that particular muscle group. I could not find a way to cheat the system at all…until we came to the exercise I dread the most: the overhead arm clap. Normally I can do about 50 four-count claps, but as we broke 100, I knew I was in for a rough time. I was at risk of losing my chem light, and I did not want to lose any points so early in the course. If I rested my arms even for one count, it would mean the end. I had to find a way to give my failing muscles a break. At about 200, I found it.

The sun had risen enough by now that I could see my fellow soldiers in the reflections of the windows on the barracks. I realized that I could keep tabs on all the SIs within our ranks by using these reflections. I was therefore able to capitalize on the precious few seconds when all the SIs happened to be looking away, and rest my broken muscles by missing a few repetitions. The first time I tried it, I was very timid, but after breaking through 300 claps, I was desperate and took advantage of every chance I got.

A voice thundered, *"You!"* I dared not look. "Yes, you! Break your chem light!" I glanced over and realized that the SI was looking toward me. *No! It can't be!* I screamed in my head. The SI walked over, and I prepared for the worst. He seemed to be heading for me, but he stopped short at the man to my immediate left. I heard the crack of the chem light and breathed out a heavy sigh of relief. I continued the hellish exercise. *It wasn't meant for you; it was meant for someone else, but that was close.* It was good that I had found a way to deal with the SIs because by the time we had finished, we had done 502 four-count overhead arm claps (that is 1004 claps above the head without stopping). After several other exercises, we moved out onto the grass and conducted Iron Mike forward lunges back and forth. It felt like my veins were pumping battery acid. The entire time, words flashed through my head: *Ridiculous! Bastards! Why?* But it always ended with *Fuck it!*

Finally…*finally*, it ended, but even after stretching and a brief cooldown, my body wasn't entirely functional. I first realized there was something wrong when I tried to bend over to pick up my canteen as soon as we finished. My insides felt knotted up. My muscles felt like they were half the size they once were, and, during any normal movement, it felt like I was tearing them apart. After another five minutes, I could hardly move. *This is the point where a normal person calls it a day and goes back to sleep. What have I gotten myself into?*

I staggered back into the barracks, barely able to maintain a walk now that all my muscle groups were effectively broken down. I unlocked my wall locker and immediately pulled out my cell phone. I scrolled through the list of names and selected John Hallet, a good friend and mentor of mine from ROTC. I began to send him a text message: "This place is…" I fumbled with my phone for a few seconds, unsure as to what word in the English language could best describe what had just happened. "This place is…crazy." I mashed the "send" button, knowing already that "crazy" was a terrible understatement and that I could not convey the significance of my situation. Frustrated, I changed and headed back outside for formation to chow, still barely able to walk, and hobbling like an old man.

We had a formation run to chow because we were running late, which seemed to happen a lot in the days to come. I felt awful as we lined up behind basic training recruits for chow. Just as I was wondering how we were going to be able to eat and still meet our time hacks, a drill sergeant yelled out, *"Make a hole! Make a hole for those Sappers…now!"* Like the Red Sea, the recruits parted and allowed us to pass between them. As we moved up the line, the drill sergeant yelled out, "Everyone here take a good look at those men! They are Sappers! Perhaps one day a few of you will be privileged to join their ranks!" On any other day, I may have felt a bit proud and carried myself a bit higher, but on this morning, I just kept my eyes straight ahead and lurched toward the front of the chow line, caring very little for the ranting of a drill sergeant.

I sat down with a plate of food. I knew that I had to eat and that food could become scarce very quickly, but for some reason, I could not eat anything. My stomach—my whole body—would not take it. I simply sat there and stared at my food. "Are you all right?" asked someone sitting next to me. I looked over and recognized Darroch (a first lieutenant, though rank is not worn while in the school). I had been right behind him during the run.

"I dunno. My insides are all knotted up…I can't eat. Nothing will go down. What should I do?" He told me to eat a banana if nothing else, and gave me his. Somehow, I forced it down and threw away everything else. However, before I did, I swiped two streusel cakes and an apple and shoved them in my pocket. No food was allowed in the barracks, but in my mind, the gloves were off and I was in survival mode. Starting at that moment, I began toying with the idea of giving up on the coveted Sapper tab and instead focusing on making it through the day. I was the "best San Diego State University could offer" to Sapper school, but the day's events had humbled me, and I began reevaluating my position and my goals for the next month. Taking food from the chow hall and hiding it in my barracks locker would play a large part in maintaining my morale. (I was not the only one who did this.) At the very least, it gave me something to do and kept my mind off the more miserable aspects of Sapper school.

The rest of the day went by slowly and was very surreal. I felt lost and out of place, like the last child to be picked up from a day-care facility, and a constant thought ran through me for the next several days: "I shouldn't be here. There must be some mistake." Nevertheless, I paid attention, stayed calm, and never stopped trying. We were introduced to the knots that I had been practicing, as well as the Swiss seat harness. We learned other skills like constructing an A-frame, a Skedco litter, and a rope bridge for a river crossing. We finished off the day with a brief on the following morning's twelve-mile foot march. And yes, we were going to have to receive, as well as insert, an IV after the march.

I think at that time I was still holding on to hope. I didn't change my goals or attitudes in the course of a single night. One of the last texts I had received from Hallet before my training started was a message from the colonel: "The colonel wanted me to tell you to kick ass." *Of course I'll kick ass*, I thought at the time. *I'm Ryan Andrew Voznick. That name and kicking ass are synonymous.* Day two's early slap across the face was rough, but I was reluctant to change outright.

The next morning we awoke at something like 0250. We had to start our foot march at 0400, and we had three hours to complete a twelve-mile march that was reported to be the most rigorous marching course the army had. (Supposedly there is one in Hawaii that is harder in terms of terrain, but is shorter.) To make matters worse, Darroch had pointed out to me before I went to sleep the night before that I had two pairs of winter boots with thick insulation on the insides. "I bet your feet feel like little ovens. Didn't your school tell you anything?" he asked.

I looked down at my boots. "No," I mumbled. "I thought it felt like that for everyone." I went to bed a bit frustrated that night.

In the morning, we formed up and moved out to our start point. I started the march confidently, but after mile three or four, I noticed that I was far less physically prepared than my peers were. I was the very *last* soldier in the entire group after the fourth mile, or so I thought. I realized I would not make the time hack, so I strolled through the rest of the course and saved my energy. This was my second deliberate act of self-preservation. As I rounded one of the corners, Staff Sergeant (SSG) Beasley, an instructor, yelled from a HMMWV (Humvee), "Hurry up, *Voznick*!" with special emphasis on the "Voznick." I quickened my pace a bit, but slowed back down as soon as he was out of sight.

I did not take my decision to slow down lightly. For some reason I found myself trying to figure out the best way to tell Hallet about what was happening. I wanted to explain my failure. I was starting out behind the curve as a cadet because I did not have any military specialty training (most of the soldiers attending were serving in infantry or engineer units), but I was even further behind the curve because I was not physically able to "hang" with the rest of the cadets. "I'm sorry," I said aloud to nobody in particular. "I'm doing the best I can. I don't know what else to do." I thought of all the kids in ROTC, my classmates. Within ROTC I would routinely speak my mind, and I always tried to stand up for what I thought was right even if it meant pissing off my superiors. I got a real kick out of that, and so I felt I had to hang in there or else I might lose that right in ROTC. I thought about Minas, Jappe, Vasquez, Hettinger, Song, Haygood, Hallet, and others there. In my mind I was letting them down. The foot march was the first big obstacle, and I was blowing it.

I thought about what my dad had told me before I left. I had admitted to him that I was a bit nervous about the twelve-mile run because I hadn't practiced for it. His reply was, "Well, you do eighty-mile desert races on your dirt bike. Those are about three hours and are pretty exhausting." True, but the difference between bike racing and military training marches was obvious. When I race I am well rested and fed, and I know that at the end of the race, I am completely done for at least two weeks. At that point in Sapper school, in addition to having almost no prior conditioning, all my muscle groups were still broken down from the hell PT and several "smoke sessions" in between. A "smoke session" is a brutal physical workout that takes anywhere between fifteen to sixty minutes. They are done as a punishment, "reward," if too much time has gone by without one, or if an instructor is feeling cheeky or bored. Though physically fit according to the army's standards, I could not keep up because I had not conditioned my body for these "smoke sessions." Regardless, as I marched I felt as if I was letting many people down, and that didn't sit well with me.

At about mile nine or ten, I heard a Humvee pull up behind me. It was SSG Beasley. "Get in, yous," he said calmly. I did not argue, and jumped into the back. It was here that I met Dues, a captain. Dues was our only female, and the first thing she said to me as I hauled myself into the back was, "Don't worry, we're gonna kill this thing on the retest at the end of camp."

"Damn right," I said with a grin. Apparently, I hadn't been the last soldier.

We picked up about three or four other stragglers and headed up to the Sapper classroom. SSG Beasley offloaded us, and then we had about five minutes or so to eat before heading into another room to administer and receive our IVs. I really hate needles, and for this exercise, I was the odd man out. I started the whole process late because they had to look for someone for me to stick. They pulled in Torres, a sergeant who was not able to attend the class I was in due to a foul-up with his paperwork. He was waiting for the next Sapper course to start, and in the meantime, he was at the beck and call of the Sapper instructors.

Torres sat down in front of me as I laid out my kit. Very slowly and nervously, I started the line. I successfully "advanced," as they say, and then SSG

Harding, who had been watching me and coaching me, suddenly went silent. I thought I had done something wrong, so I pulled the whole thing out.

"What the fuck are you doing, Sapper? You had it," SSG Harding said coolly. "Now you have to do his other arm." I apologized to Torres, who was a real sport about the whole thing. I had no problem at all with the second attempt.

After we were finished, everyone started moving outside. I started to gear up and asked the medic if I really needed to have an IV. The medic answered with a shocked look and said enthusiastically, "Yes. Everyone *has* to have one!" The medic himself hooked me up quickly, and then the SIs ordered me to squeeze my saline bag as hard as I could. I could feel the freezer-cooled liquid enter my vein. The harder I squeezed, the more of the vein I could feel due to the chilled liquid in the IV bag. The real reason for the IV was to replenish and revive our bodies a bit because there was still a whole day of training—and smoke sessions.

We were led outside and began practicing buddy rappel seats. Apparently, we were going to jump off a ninety-foot cliff with a buddy on our backsides, so we needed to learn how to tie ourselves in properly. There were no harnesses. We only used the rope that we were issued, which meant our rappels were far from comfortable and usually left bruises.

After a few hours of training, it was lunchtime. Mermite chow (food kept in large containers for warmth) was brought out to us, and we were hurried through the line. Usually there was not enough time to eat an entire meal, so we just ate as much as we could. The SIs decided to have a little fun and put out the order to eat every bit of food in fifteen minutes. We rushed the table, and everyone loaded up their plates with food, but I could already tell it was hopeless. I knew the standard. If at any time during Sapper school we did not complete the assigned task to time or standard, a good, hard smoke session always followed. And the SIs don't bullshit around with their smoke sessions; they are brutal.

As I wolfed down my food, I wondered if they were seriously going to smoke us right after eating. If this had happened on the last day of Sapper school, the answer would have been obvious, but at this point, I was still naïve. "*Stop!*" yelled one of the SIs. "Get out onto the road—two lines facing in!" he continued. We ran out onto the road and got into double-arm interval, which meant any hope of *not* being smoked was out the window. They started us on side straddle hops, then moved to push-ups, and then to mountain climbers. After we were thoroughly beaten, the SIs ordered us to run a lap around the training area. Then we did two more because "we weren't moving fast enough." In between the runs, they continued to PT everyone, obviously trying to get someone to vomit. Finally, after about twenty minutes or so, they had us return to training.

The dirty fucks! I thought as this was happening. *What the fuck is this? I thought we were supposed to learn something here. Sure, it was supposed to be tough, but this is asinine! We're being treated like dogs—like shit! Fuck this!*

All these thoughts and others like them were quietly contained within me for the rest of the school session. Expressing my frustration would have served no purpose whatsoever. I quietly "sucked it up," as they say, and carried on. I never cared for fraternities and thus never joined one, but here I felt like a pledge forced to do ridiculous things while the seniors laughed. At that point, I began to get pissed: pissed that I had been set up for failure, pissed that nobody had told me what to expect, pissed that no one had attempted to help me beyond getting me into the school. I was also pissed at myself because in the depths of my mind, in the dark recesses, I was actually trying to think of a way home, a way out, if there was any way possible.

CHAPTER THREE
General Studies Phase

"Sapper, how about you fall back in and keep training."

The following morning we woke up and moved out to conduct waterborne operations. By this time, it was obvious that getting three or four hours of sleep at night was the routine. The packet I had received said that the normal training day was from 0500–2200. This was a complete fallacy. Not once was that "timeline" adhered to. It could be considered a *good* day if you slept four hours the night before.

My squad was assigned as the ADVON (work party) for the move to the lake, and thus we had to wake up about an hour before everyone else. We loaded up a pair of M1088 transports (basically glorified dump trucks) with the platoon's gear, and then jumped in ourselves. Normally, sitting in the back of these canvas-covered trucks was so uncomfortable that sleep was impossible. On this ride, however, I managed to crawl over our gear and onto our A bags, which were loaded with fresh changes of clothing. I sprawled out and slept for the entire hour-and-a-half-or-so drive to the lake. When we got there, we set up the training area. After the rest of the platoon arrived, we conducted what could be considered the "fun part" of Sapper school: helocasting.

Helocasting involves jumping from a helicopter (for us a Chinook) into a body of water in full gear. It's pretty simple, really. You just walk out the back ramp of the helicopter, chuck your ruck out, and then jump after it. The part that adds a bit of excitement is that you're moving along at about fifteen miles per hour at an altitude of about thirty feet when you go in.

We did two jumps that morning. As was the case several times at Sapper school, just as I thought things were finally starting to even out, they got far, far worse. We had to endure more brutal smoke sessions and asinine punishments. Most of the remaining day was spent having our muscle groups broken down once again. This time they had us walk out into the lake water until we were about knee deep. They conducted all the same exercises as we would do on any normal PT, and had no problem using a jet ski or boat to create waves. These waves would cause problems for anyone who was not wary while doing sit-ups or push-ups, and a lot of us drank an unhealthy amount of lake water. In addition, several of the instructors would splash water into our individual faces using small, orange lifeguard buoys. After about an hour or so of this, we were told to swim across the lake and back in half an hour. The catch was that we had to tie ourselves to a buddy as well as both our rucksacks. Being completely exhausted, several of the groups foundered during this task. The instructors' response was to ride boats around the slower groups and "encourage" them verbally. They also rode their boats around us to keep the water moccasins away...or so they said.

After completing that task and arriving back on shore, we formed up and fell out for classroom exercises. It soon became apparent that not every-one was doing well physically. About half of us (not including myself) were throwing up lake water. After twenty or thirty minutes of this, there were two or three people still vomiting—and there was blood in their puke. In the movies, if somebody is throwing or coughing up blood, it usually means they're done for. My friend Yanak was one of those vomiting blood. In addi-tion to the blood, he was having difficulty breathing. He asked my advice, and I said, "There is nothing here that is worth permanent damage." After a little while longer, he finally conceded that he needed to get some help. After all, according to the papers, we were entitled to one twenty-four-hour period of medical recovery if absolutely necessary. In Yanak's case, this seemed the only option. I offered to go with him, and stood by quietly as Yanak pre-sented his case to SSG Harding.

"Sergeant, I'm coughing up blood…and it's really hard to breathe."

SSG Harding stood erect with his arms across his chest. His sunglasses obscured his eyes, and at first he refused to move or acknowledge our presence. This made for an intimidating picture.

Yanak continued, "I don't want to quit or anything, but I just think that at this point, I can't carry on anymore and—"

"Sapper," SSG Harding said coldly and quietly, cutting Yanak off, "how about you fall back in and keep training." There was a brief, awkward pause, and then Yanak continued, unable to hide the intimidation in his voice.

"I don't think I should. I mean…I don't want to quit…but I can't breathe, and I'm coughing up blood…"

"Sapper, if you fall out now, you won't get your tab. If the medics pull you out of training, they aren't going to be able to get you back out here in twenty-four hours and you will fail this school. So fall back in and keep training."

There was a long pause, and Yanak finally answered with a feeble, "OK." We returned to the formation and continued our instruction.

The best I could offer was a crappy, "Hang in there," and "If things get worse, go *tell* him that you need to see the medics and go to the hospital." Fortunately, Yanak's condition improved slightly as the day wore on, partially due to no more smokings for the rest of that day or night. We kept training until midnight, when they finally fed us. (It had been a full twelve hours since our last meal—a bit of training for the real food deprivation that was to come.) We racked out at 0100, took a brief two-hour nap, and woke up at 0300 for what was called "boat PT."

There was no time to change into a new uniform, and we ran down to the shore. For the first hour, the SIs had us do exercises utilizing the Kodiak boats, such as boat push-ups, boat presses, and others I don't care to remember. After again reaching muscle failure, the SIs ordered us to carry the boats above our heads down a road that skirted part of the lake. The instructors had us race against the other boats, but stopped us frequently on our journey to have us drop the boats and do more boat PT.

After a mile or so, I was experiencing muscle failure bad enough that I was struggling just to keep the boat above my head. I was also located at the front of the boat, and everybody could see my predicament. At first there was mild encouragement from those behind me. (On a side note, the Kodiak boat is heavy, especially when it's loaded with water jugs, oars, and other gear.) As we entered the second mile, however, the tone of my "mates" began to change. Instead of a somewhat friendly "Come on, Voznick, you got this!" I began hearing comments more along the lines of "What the fuck is wrong with you? Keep the boat above your *goddamn* head!" Truly, I had never in my life been the weak link. Never before had *I* been the one unable to shoulder a burden, but that morning I, once again, had a very humbling experience. The shouts and curses from my peers did nothing to cure my broken muscles, but I did the best I could.

The situation reached a new low when the SI who was spotting our boat ordered us to stop, and told each of us to break our chem lights. We were losing the race, and so we were being punished. Naturally, I was the target of the blame, but I became numb and ignored the swearing. I forfeited my right to speak in any jovial manner with anyone for the next few days. I would have to earn back respect among my peers before I could consider that. There was nothing I could do. I was not physically conditioned for this. I was doing better than the best I could do, and I found solace in that, and a reason to shrug off the comments of my peers.

Somehow, I managed to finish a third mile before the SIs stopped us in front of a stagnant pool of water, an inlet adjacent to the lake. The SIs ordered us to place the boats on the ground, much to my relief. After we had set them down, they ordered us into this disgusting water. Once we had waded in about waist deep, one of the SIs called out, "What we're going to do now is something I like to call the Bellagio." For the next fifteen minutes or so, the SIs guffawed and laughed as they had us crouch low and spring up into the air, apparently like the fountains at the Bellagio casino in Las Vegas. It was degrading and absolutely stupid. I could not understand the purpose of this exercise, but my mind was so numb at that point that I simply didn't care about anything anymore. I had nothing left to lose, nothing at all. I was tired, cold, hungry, wet, suffered muscle failure several times, and had been singled out as the weak link, as the shit bag. The only thing I had on my side was my general health, and I found myself wishing—hoping—that the putrid, frigid water I was submerged in would cause hypothermia, sending me home. To me, hypothermia was a legitimate excuse; otherwise, I would be damned if I was going to give up. Despite the shock of realizing how unprepared I was, I wasn't going to throw in the towel, no matter what they did. The frustration and anger I felt only strengthened my resolve.

The water didn't give me hypothermia, and we were soon ordered back to the boats to finish off another grueling mile with the boat above our heads. This time, however, each boat carried an instructor. They picked up the ropes attached to the boats and would jump up and down screaming, "Yhaaa!" while slapping the "reins." Incredibly, over time my muscles got used to it—or something. Sure, the pain was still there, but my arms were doing what I was telling them to do now, even though they had hit muscle failure repeatedly. After we finished the last mile, we were ordered to place our boats near the shore and face a hillside with a steep, muddy slope.

One of the instructors showed us how to conduct a prisoner crawl. This involves placing your hands in the small of your back and bending your knees so that your hands touch your feet, similar to being hog-tied. The SIs then laughed and laughed as they ordered us up the side of the hill. Mud caked our uniforms and our bodies. My knees were rubbed raw, and mud got into my mouth. I looked left and right and realized everyone was having the same problems. After about fifteen minutes of this, the SIs finally ordered us into the boats, and we rowed back to our start point alongside the lake. After getting back to shore, we loaded up the M1088s and headed back to the barracks. We were given a few minutes (literally) to change, and then were ordered to the classroom.

We finished off the day with a weapons familiarization class and exam. We learned how to take apart and reassemble the AK-47, and how to identify different machine guns and rifles commonly used by our enemies. This was the only part of Sapper school that I truly enjoyed. We were encouraged to pick up and handle all sorts of weapons. Some of my favorites were the PPSh-41, the Sten gun, the DShK, and the various RPGs. I passed the tests well enough, and I believe we were released at a decent time that night, perhaps at 2200 or 2300.

One thing I do remember clearly was that chow was delivered to us again that night. Wrapped Fig Newtons were part of that meal, and while we were cleaning up, I crammed about six of them in my pockets. I went back to the barracks that night and started creating a stockpile of food that would swell over the next few days. It included streusel cakes, Nutri-Grain bars, Fig Newtons, apples, and even a whole MRE (ready-to-eat meal). Any chance I could get, I swiped food and hid it. I made sure to take a snack with me every morning. In this way, I never went hungry again until entering the field.

I was as discreet in my consumption of the goods as I was when I stashed them. Typically, I would just go to the restroom and grab a quick bite while I took a piss in a stall. Other times I would simply wait for an opportunity when nobody was looking. I never was caught, neither by friend nor by foe, because I did all of it under the radar. The Sapper instructors were in some respects "the enemy," and I would fight them with all I had. (I'll get into that a bit later.) I wasn't the only one who did this, but I may have been the one who did it the most. The hellish experience of the boat PT and the hazing were enough in my mind to chuck all the rules and "fight back" any way I could. The gloves were off, and I had to keep myself propped up any way I could—and damn all, I was going to do it.

CHAPTER FOUR
Before the Field

"Are you a cool guy back home, Voznick?"

The grueling training continued day after day. We had a five-mile run the next morning—which, unlike the first PT, was actually not so bad (in Sapper school terms). After the run, those of us who finished on time (seven minutes per mile) were allowed to return to the barracks so long as we could climb the thirty-foot rope. Rope climbing was somewhat difficult for me under normal circumstances, but as I rose to the top of the rope, I was chafing my legs. The pain from that combined with muscle failure was too much. As soon as I tagged the top, I *slid* back down, causing bad blisters on both hands. One of them actually ripped open and oozed out blood. There was intense, sharp pain in my hands for the rest of the day.

I was extremely pissed at myself for having failed at one of my primary goals of Sapper school: self-preservation. I would now have to cradle this wound through the rest of training. There would be no first aid or favoritism from the instructors, and the reason for this would be explained in due time. In the meantime, I took the best care of myself that I could.

We spent the rest of that day on demolitions calculations, and the next few days came and went quickly. We learned the proper formulas for and use of certain types of explosives, including TNT, C-4, and dynamite. One day we moved out to the demolitions site and prepared for another overnight training event.

The demolitions range was interesting. We were given classroom exercises on how to construct field-expedient demolitions. Among these were platter charges, shaped charges, satchel charges, crater charges, grapeshot, soapbox claymores, and door charges. After the classes, we were ordered outside, where blocks of TNT, dynamite, C-4 plastic explosives, and detonators were organized on several tables. We were then told to construct at least two of the various explosives we had just been taught. There was a touch of comedy about this whole situation. The idea of about ten guys crowded around a table under a Quonset hut, cutting, molding, and building bombs was too much for me.

"Funny, I used to build birdhouses in Boy Scouts at summer camps under huts like these," I said aloud, "and now I'm shoving C-4 in the bottom of a Folgers coffee can, learning how to make grapeshot and other ways to kill people. Oh, the times they are a changin'." There was some laughter.

After helping create the grapeshot, a platter charge, and a saline bag door charge, I moved out with the others to the demolitions range. We were told to place our explosives (all except the door charges) and retreat to several bunkers at the far end of the range. We could not see anything inside the bunkers, but we felt and heard the explosions. After the last of the bombs went off, we went back outside and examined our work. We had put a lot of holes in the ground and completely demolished one of the containers that had been left on the range.

That night I was made squad leader, and a conversation came up about how much time everyone had put into preparing for the school. The average was about four to six months, with some claiming they had been training for a whole year. I was dumbfounded.

"Hey, Voznick," someone asked, "how long did you take to get ready?"

"About a week and a half, dude," I replied quickly. There was a moment of silence.

"What the *fuck*? Are you serious, Voznick?"

"Yeah, really, I am. I put in my application in January, and they told me two weeks before the start date that I was going. When I asked too many questions, they said it was an army school and not to worry about it." There was another moment of silence as everyone within earshot listened to my story. Then they all burst out laughing.

"Ha ha ha! Oh shit, seriously? Well, that explains a lot! Ha ha ha!"

The story spread and soon everyone knew. They began recounting that morning in the chow hall when I could not eat. "Did you guys see his face that day? Ha ha ha! Jeez, you really had no idea how it was going to be, huh, Voznick? Ha ha ha!"

I humbly laughed along with them, but over the next few days, the laughter subsided a bit and was replaced with a form of respect. That I had not been trained up or even told what to expect was enough for most people to realize that despite my handicap, I was still here and moving forward. I heard more and more compliments such as, "Hey, man, good fucking job hanging in there." This probably also had something to do with the fact that I was getting stronger and more acclimated each day, and was thus able to keep up a little better. I was glad that the ice had broken a bit, and I maintained a pessimistic/humorous attitude that entertained my buddies and kept my own spirits up.

The next morning we had a five-mile boot run, which was a nightmare. It was by far the toughest run I had done in my life. It's not worth describing. It was simply very tough and very painful. Experiences like this—"the toughest," "the longest," "the hardest," "the most impossible"—were typical of every single day of Sapper school. Descriptions of any one of these events could fill several pages, but for readability, I'm condensing these events. Suffice it to say, every day had new, hardening experiences.

After the run, we spent the rest of the day on breaching. Simply put, breaching is knocking down or blowing down doors. We practiced with "hoodlum" tools, such as a battering ram and a device that looks like a crowbar on steroids. We spent some hands-on time with the hoodlum tools, and then used the various door charges we had created at the demolitions range. Everyone had to blow down a door and, as I said earlier, the instructions on how to do anything were usually stated once—then never again.

This was the case when I was told to blow down a door using my water charge. The water charge has the highest standoff. In other words, it's a big bomb, and so you have to stand way back when it blows. I had an assistant help me wire the thing after I placed it on the door. We rolled the wire back to the side of the building, and my buddy gave me two cylinders that looked like Pez dispensers with two loops coming out the top of each one. "What the fuck do I do with this?" I whispered. I was being graded, so he couldn't say much. I stuck my fingers through the loops of what appeared to be the detonators (Pez dispensers). *OK…hmm…in the movies they push down on 'em.* I pushed down hard but nothing happened. I tried again, and still nothing. I tried twisting them. I kept it up until I finally said, "Fuck it." I turned around and started to stand. I still had my fingers in the loops.

Booooooooom!

I flew backward, more from shock than the actual explosion, and landed on my ass. After clearing the building, my squad came back out laughing. The instructor thought I had "hesitated," but I actually just had no idea what I was doing.

I was the only guy in the platoon from California, or even the West Coast for that matter, and after this my buddies started poking fun at me. "Hey, maaaan," Baker said with a hippie accent. "What's going on, maaaan? Wanna get high, maaaan?" I laughed and even got into character every now and then.

Afterward, we headed back to the classroom for our land navigation briefing and partner assignments. This course was rumored to be one of the tougher courses in the army. Land navigation started at 0300 the following day. My partner was a young, somewhat immature West Pointer. He incessantly talked up his land navigation abilities, and I reassured him of my own. However, when he tried to plot our start point, he missed the grid square. That was the only time he would ever plot a point during our land navigation. He was very quiet after that snafu, and I didn't ask for his help. I simply took over the plotting for our team.

We had to find the points in order; in other words, they gave us the first point at 0300 (the start time) but only the first point. We had to find that first point to get the coordinates for our second point, and so on. This was the most interesting land navigation course I'd ever been through. Within the first fifteen minutes, Bailey, my partner, stepped on a chicken or some other bird creature. The bird gave off a weird, monotonic noise and ran off.

As we carried on, I noticed my partner was unique in his land navigation technique. He refused to use a pace count or a compass, or even a protractor for that matter. His method was strictly terrain association, which annoyed me considerably. We could not see anything during the first few hours of morning, and, despite my best efforts at convincing him otherwise, he insisted that I follow him. After a few wrong turns, I told him in no uncertain terms that I didn't have much faith in the method we were using—until he found the first point, a post in the ground with a symbol that we transposed onto our grade sheet. I was awestruck. I'm still convinced there was a lot of luck involved in finding that first point, and as we moved out to the second, I maintained my calculations to counter any wrong turns he might make.

We found the intersection we wanted to use as our attack point, or the staging point used before going off into the woods to look for the post. Before we moved out to search, I insisted on two things: (1) I was going to shoot an azimuth, a compass heading that would keep us on track, and (2) I was going to drop my rucksack. He didn't have a problem with the first, and only commented on the second. "Well, just make sure it's off the road and hidden well." At this point I was still having a lot of trouble rucking, and although the rule was not to remove our ruck, I wasn't going to break down my body if I could help it. Thankfully, nothing came of this little deviation. Within ten minutes, we found the second point.

The third, fourth, and fifth points came and went, but those points involved a tough struggle. My partner, a self-proclaimed woodsman from Vermont, regaled me with stories about hikes through the woods as a kid. He rattled on and on, even when I was exhausted and fell behind. "C'mon, Voznick," he would yell back, "you got this!" This kid could move like a deer and made me feel like a damn tortoise. My only counterargument was that he did not even once "handle" a road, instead preferring to "cross country" or "dead reckon" to our points. This led to exhaustive climbing, slipping, and falling through the woods. While going up a hill, I grabbed a branch for support. When it slipped out of my hands, a hundred ticks that had apparently been residing on the branch and leaves sprayed down onto me. I brushed off as many as I could, but as time went on, I could feel some of them crawling up and down my back, mixing with the drenching sweat so that I could not distinguish one from the other. There was no time to strip down and clean up. What misery.

Sometimes I had to rope my partner in and let him know that we weren't in the position that he thought we were. In these incidents, he would stare at the map where I was pointing and then say something like, "Oh…yeah…OK…OK. I see where we need to go. C'mon." I would roll my eyes behind his back, but I didn't complain because the system he was using—for some damn reason—actually worked. We finished the course after getting five out of six points (we only needed four). Nobody in the platoon got six points, and only one other team got five. I felt pretty good about this (even though I was completely exhausted) because if there is one thing I can do—or should be able to do—it's read a map and compass and do well on an army land navigation course. (Historically, I had never missed a point on any official army land navigation course.) Of course, much credit goes to my partner.

Before we left, we were pretty badly smoked at the conclusion of land navigation because we had arrived at the site late that morning (we started at something like 0307 instead of 0300). We headed back to the classroom and received IED (improvised explosive devices) identification training for the rest of the evening. This was nothing too spectacular, except that we watched some gruesome videos of IED explosions.

The following day was all rappelling and climbing. Our training aid for this was a forty-five-foot tower. Climbing up this giant was a task in itself. There was no stairway, only a large ladder. Once on top, we would be rappelling off two faces. One side had a wall all the way down and one had nothing, just open air. First, we rappelled off either side Hollywood-style (no gear) and then with forty-pound rucks. These were pretty easy. The twist to this whole exercise was that we were expected to tie ourselves into the ropes. We were being tested, and we had mere seconds to complete the assigned rappel before we were failed for not moving fast enough.

The grand finale was an "Aussie" rappel: a face-first plunge off of the open-air side of the tower. If done right, you look a lot like Tom Cruise in *Mission Impossible*. The instructors once again decided to entertain themselves. They had people sing songs or yell out the Sapper creed while they were in the jump position, which means they were horizontal facing the ground. Only the rope tucked into your chest is keeping you from falling, and the arm that holds it becomes tired very quickly.

I had planned to do my best impersonation of Axl Rose in "Welcome to the Jungle," but on my jump, as I lowered myself into position and felt the muscle strain begin to burn in my arm, one of the instructors yelled out, "Oh, my God! *Fuck!* His shit is loose; the knot is popping out! *Get him back in here!*"

Another instructor yelled out, "Voznick, grab my hand!"

After about two seconds, I instinctively knew this was a joke. In fact, without any exaggeration, if my rope had broken and I had fallen face first to my death, I probably would not have made a single sound of panic. I simply did not care anymore. I was too tired to care about *anything* except what I was being told to do or whatever task lay directly in my path. Lack of sleep and the constant training had done what, I assume, was intended: if I could not control something, it didn't matter. Emotion, desire, and, most definitely, *fear* were totally gone. I played their game, however, because I knew that if I did this right, they would know who I was—they would know that I was the guy they screwed with and got a good laugh from. When I hit muscle failure, I put on my best fake-terrified face ever and fell the forty or so feet before catching myself and touching ground. I did not panic or screw up my descent by grabbing the rope with my free hand. When I landed, the instructors and some of my buddies were laughing hysterically. I took it in stride and knew that I had banked some points with the instructors. They had screwed with me more than anyone else, and for the next couple of days, whenever they saw me, there was more joking than yelling. This little event made life slightly easier.

The afternoon was spent learning how to scale back up the two sides of the tower. We learned how to tie up a fairly simple system of ropes and scale the wall side. On the open-air side, we received a piece of equipment that resembled a staple gun: a jumar. I hooked myself into the staple gun and began creeping up to the top of the tower. In both climbs, the motion was similar to stretching your arms upward, moving your legs into the fetal position, and then repeating the process. As I neared the top and my staple gun hit the bottom of the tower top, I brain farted. For some reason (sleep deprivation?), I had zoned out on how to dismount the contraption. I looked up into the face of one of the instructors. "Uh, sergeant, how do I get off this thing?"

"How do you think you should get off?" he replied, sounding pissed off. I looked away from him for about a second for no reason, and then he blurted out, "Sapper, get up here now! We got training to do and you're *fucking it up!*"

Robotically, I started unhooking my straps even before the words left his mouth. He flinched for a second, seeing that I really didn't know what I was doing, but he held back. Another instructor peered over the sergeant's shoulder to watch. I cannot recall exactly what I did, but I know I unhooked everything until I was only holding on to the device with my free hands. *If only Mom and Dad could see this.* I didn't give a shit about whatever procedure I was supposed to follow; the guy said to get up and I was going to do it. I began by grabbing the top of the tower and then swinging my legs up onto the top. I was treating this thing as if I were a kid climbing a tree. The instructor flinched for a second time, but again held back and simply watched. I was completely confident in myself and knew I was not going to fall; otherwise, I wouldn't have done it. It was not, however, the correct way of dismounting.

The other instructor who was watching yelled out, "Holy *fuck*, *look* at this guy!"

"Voznick? Look, he has no damn facial expression! Are you a cool guy back home, Voznick? I bet you're a cool guy!" He said this in a contemptuous tone, but it did not even register that the sergeant had been yelling at me until I was safely on top of the tower. "Good job, cool guy. Now get off the *damn tower*," he said. For some time afterward, he and other instructors referred to me as "cool guy."

The following day was cliff day. There are not too many interesting things to say about this day other than it was a big test day. I did fairly well, collecting probably about 70 percent of the points offered that day. The cliff site was located in a dense part of the woods. The cliff itself was a ninety-foot vertical drop, which may have made for some harrowing rappels—but, like I said earlier, somehow I just did not have much energy (or whatever) left to spend on fear. At this point, for me it was just another day to get through.

At lunch, the Rangers in our unit were pulled out and taken down to the creek bed. There wasn't much water running in that creek, but it was particularly muddy. The SIs had the Rangers recite their creed. It started well, but whenever one of them got out of sync, the SIs smoked them all pretty bad. After about ten or fifteen minutes of this, the Rangers were caked in wet mud from head to toe (they were literally forced to roll around in the mud).

My buddy, First Lieutenant (1LT) Darroch, was one of them. He came back and started eating chow with me, but because they were the last to start eating, they all had the worst MREs: the omelet. MREs are all basically dog food, but the omelet is the worst. Still, Darroch took it all in stride and very quickly showed me how the omelet meal could be improved and made edible. He maintained himself despite his obvious physical misery. After all that we had been through, after being hazed, how he could still manage to crack a smile was astonishing. At one point, he said to me, "Voznick, it's all about keeping a sense of humor. When we get out into the field especially, it's going to suck and everyone knows that. A sense of humor is really the only thing that can help out there." We talked a little during the five minutes we had to eat, and then we were ordered to continue our training. The yelling, cursing, and everything else you could think of that was associated with this training continued for the rest of that day.

The next day was the twelfth day of training, and involved our last graded run. Again, this was a tough run, but by then my body was well conditioned, and I withstood the strain just fine. Our knots test was also that day, and I did fairly well. Fortunately for me, my grader was SSG Wayne. SSG Wayne was one of the instructors whom I actually appreciated not solely out of fear. He was the "explosives guy," and looked and acted the part of the kind of crazy bomb guy from the movies. At the demolitions range, I got to talking with him about napalm. My argument was that the ingredients we were taught to use did not create the "inextinguishable homemade napalm" that he said it did. He was intrigued by the fact that I had heard of this before Sapper school, and we talked for about fifteen minutes about the napalm mixture. When he graded me on knots that day, he was somewhat lenient on a few, and I did well overall. The rest of that day and the following were spent on other various tests. Some time was spent turning over control of the school to the patrolling instructors because after day thirteen, GE (General Education) phase was over, and the field training would begin.

On the fourteenth day of training, we woke up early to start a four-mile ruck run with a group of new instructors. This was a ruck run with forty pounds in our packs excluding equipment. There were four squads, and each squad was ordered to carry two M249 light machine guns and an M240. Although the task was once again brutal, the four-mile run seemed to end quickly enough. However, once we returned to the start point, we were smoked and messed up pretty bad. The new instructors had to establish themselves, and so I don't blame them. Suffice it to say that by the end of the session, we were thoroughly exhausted, drenched in water, and caked in mud from several "prisoner crawls" while being sprayed with hoses. But this wasn't far from the standard routine for a day at Sapper school.

At or around this time, I suffered another injury. We were doing some PT training and I was a "casualty." Ramirez picked me up and threw me on his back. I was doing fine at first, but as he ran and I gently bounced up and down on his back, my left nut slipped between his back and his ruck. Suddenly it felt like I was being jackhammered. "Wait, stop. Ow! Dude, stop…stop stop stop stop stop…*stooooooop*! *Ahhhhhhhhhhhhhhhhhhhh!*"

I screamed like a chick in a horror movie. As my nut was being pulverized, I suddenly felt a warm sensation in my crotch. When Ramirez finally threw me off his back (because we had arrived at the destination, not because of my screams), my whole platoon was laughing. *I've lost a testicle…it's shattered…it's gone…I'm done.* It's hard to describe the feeling of not thinking but *knowing* that you've lost one of your boys. I lay on the ground for a few minutes, and then finally got up and hobbled around. The medic checked my junk and told me I had probably "burst a vessel," and to continue training unless it swelled up a lot. *Well, that figures.* Problems from this injury continued until the very last day of Sapper school.

The rest of that day was spent on classroom and field exercises. We had to learn a rather complex and exhaustive way of delivering an operations order (OPORD), the written orders used by the army to initiate an operation. It was so comprehensive and so vast that I believe it is quite impossible to memorize the methods and terminology in their entirety, especially when one is *at best* at 70 percent mental and physical strength because of the constant sleep and food deprivations. Regardless, for that day and the following two days, we practiced and rehearsed battle drills and this revised OPORD.

Then it began to rain. Thus far it had not "rained" in a way that had made things miserable. That day, however, it came down in buckets. We had a West Pointer as platoon leader (PL) and an eighteen-year-old specialist as our platoon sergeant (PSG) in charge that day (students rotate leadership positions at Sapper school). When we were told to move outside to conduct training on battle drills, everyone in the platoon chimed in that we should put on our wet weather gear. The West Pointer and the eighteen-year old stared at each other. Then the West Pointer looked back at us and yelled, "No wet weather gear!" So that was it. *Fucking moron.* We ran out there, and within minutes, we were thoroughly soaked. Unfortunately, there was no lightning, which would have stopped outdoor training at least momentarily. Nope, this rain came down thick as mud. It was so thick it felt as if you could actually inhale water if you weren't careful. Perhaps even worse was the wind. At a certain point, it seemed that gale-force winds came from nowhere and battered us for hours.

And we trained.

My teeth rattled and muscles quivered. It lasted the entire day, and there was no respite except for an hour when we listened to some damn general speak. The instructors had not planned for his speech in our training and so had not scheduled time for it. Therefore, that general's speech cut into our sleep for that night. This was probably the worst and lowest point for me at Sapper school. One of the guys, Romo, actually turned the heat up in the classroom during the general's speech, and he was punished for it, but we were thankful. Romo was one of the few who became a Sapper, I'm happy to say.

The hell day turned to a hell night and then into a hell morning. We finished the day's tasks at about 0230 the following day. Instead of being released to our barracks, we received one of many demoralization speeches from our new instructors. Of all the new things I was experiencing, this was the most baffling. We were sitting in the room with a couple of the SIs who were just bullshitting with us, not really talking about anything in particular, when they would work themselves up into a rage and then punish us. They would be talking about what it means to be a Sapper, and then say how none of us deserved it, or how we would all screw our buddies or something to that effect, and then they would just blow their tops. "Beat your *fucking faces*!" they would yell. "You think you can do a few months of training and then come here and expect to succeed?" These unprovoked tirades happened several times during those few days before the actual field exercises. At about 0330 they finally released us.

We went into the back room, and the platoon decided that we would not go back to our barracks but instead sleep in the formation room to be up at 0500. I was wet, miserable, tired, cold, hungry, exhausted, and a whole slew of other things, but I did not agree with them. I got it worked out with a buddy, and we left the classroom and headed back to the barracks by ourselves. When we got there, I had a nice long, hot shower, ate from my "inventory," and changed into a clean, fresh uniform. Though I knew that in an hour I would be back in the same crap, what I was experiencing was the closest thing to total freedom at that school, and the tradeoff in sleep was worth it. Nobody really knew where we were or what we were doing, and so I took advantage of the luxury of leisure time. Ramirez and I ambled back to the classroom, eating pizza someone had stored in their locker and shooting the shit. It was all so surreal, and I had never felt so free since leaving Chino. When we got back, we rolled out on the ground and got about forty-five minutes worth of sleep. The next day wasn't much different except that the rain was gone, and we were released at a somewhat decent time (I believe 2300 or 2400 at night).

Mental strain is a funny thing. It breaks you down gradually, and, without any real conscious thought, one can become extremely sorry for oneself. I had done my best to fight it off, and training kept us busy most of the time anyway, but any and every night that I could, I would call either John Hallet or my dad to help keep me going. These conversations, though I can't recall most of them, were like a bit of gas for an engine that was running on fumes. The night after the rain, I called my dad and described the last two days to him. "I don't know what to say," he said. "I'm sorry you had to go through that, Ryan."

I don't recall exactly how I brought it up or exactly what I said, but it went something like this: "I don't want to let anyone down...and there are a lot of good people in the program that expect good things from me. I usually shoot my mouth off most of the time, and I think that if I go back there without the tab that...well...that they might think a little less of me."

There was a moment of silence. The reply was electric. "*You* don't have to impress *them*! Who gives a *damn* what they think of you! *They're* not the ones out there, *you* are. None of us here are going to think less of you. Just get through it and get home. From what you've told me, it sounds like those people don't care about you, so just watch out for yourself and get back in one piece. *Who the hell cares what anyone else thinks?*"

I couldn't let go of those words. After hanging up and walking back to the barracks, I felt a lot better. Within Army ROTC, I'm Ryan Voznick, the guy with an "I don't give a damn" and "who gives a shit what people think about me" attitude. Up to that point I had given everything I had to the task at hand. The past doesn't matter and the future should only be planned to the point where it doesn't interfere with present circumstances. I knew this. I guess I just needed someone to remind me given my state of mind. At that point I completely stopped caring about the school and the tab. My goals were (1) don't screw over my buddies, (2) take care of my buddies, and (3) take care of myself because nothing is worth permanent damage. (These were subconscious thoughts at the time, not something I actually determined literally.) On the morning of the sixteenth day of training at Sapper school, we packed up our gear and moved out into the woods of Fort Leonard Wood to begin our field training exercise, or FTX.

CHAPTER FIVE
The Field

"At its worst, it's the feeling of being sick with a cold and hung over at the same time."

When breakfast was brought out, the instructors gave us a bit more time than usual to consume our food. This would be day one of the field and the first day of gradual food deprivation. We ate until we felt we would burst and then we ate more because we knew they would never tell us when we would eat again…ever. That day was spent in the field but only in classroom settings, primarily conducting SERE training (survival training). We also conducted Military Operations in Urban Terrain (MOUT), this time with paintball guns.

I was the point man for one of the room-clearing teams, and as we stacked outside one of the rooms, a hand popped out of the door holding a paintball gun. I was staring down the barrel of the enemy gun when I hesitated. I have played many paintball/airsoft games, and "blind fire" is not allowed. Neither is shooting someone at such close range. I could have shot this man's hands easily, and very nearly did so. I did not because I felt that if I did, I would be punished by the SIs. I paid for that when the gun in front of me fired, and four or five rounds stitched paintballs up my thigh and stomach—more bruises to nurse through the field. To add insult to injury, the SIs gave me a hard time for "hesitating."

We were not fed a lunchtime meal on that first day. Later in the evening, we moved a ways into the woods to a small, isolated compound. This would be our "base camp" during refit in the field. I managed to keep a small journal during my time in the field. To a small degree, it helped me maintain my sense of self, and I knew that it would probably prove invaluable if I decided to write a story about my experience. Due to the nature of the field training and the dreamlike state I finally ended up in, I'm glad I did. The entries in italics are the actual word-for-word entries. I have followed up each entry with descriptions of the day's highlights to try to convey fully what the Sapper school FTX is like.

6/16–6/17

First day was easy. We had a huge breakfast in the morning before we left. No lunch but in the evening we had an MRE, and I felt better than I have since I got here. Package came through today but had to turn it over to the cadre. Got the gum* and first aid out though. It's helping out here in day two a lot, but I have to conserve it. Four o'clock right now and I feel hungry. Fortunately, I got a solid six hours of sleep last night. The situation is going to deteriorate rapidly. Sleep deprivation starts tonight, and they say we will eat but only for eight minutes. Moving out soon. This is going to suck.
Six hours/zero hours (two meals)

The asterisk after "gum" I placed in the journal to help remind me of a certain incident that happened. The reason I did not write it in the journal was for fear of its capture and confiscation. If that had occurred, I was sure that I would be smoked indefinitely and worse if the SIs had discovered what I had done with the package. Here is what happened.

For some inexplicable reason, at the end of day one, I finally received a package in the mail that I had expected within the first few days of my arrival. Why they delivered a large box to me out in the field, I'll never comprehend. Nobody else received any mail in the field. Inside I knew there was a dozen PowerBars and chewing gum with some blister treatment stuff I had long ago requested from home. I told Yarborough, an ex-staff private first class at Sapper school, and he and I made plans to sneak the entire box under the driver's seat of one of our dump truck transports. He backed out at the last second, however, so I grudgingly turned over the box of goodies to the instructors…or at least I tried to.

When I showed it to the instructors, they eyed me suspiciously even though I opened it for the first time in front of them. Then the most unbelievable thing happened: they told me to take it back to my ruck and hang on to it for a few hours until we were back at the base camp. That was it for me. If you put a plate of food in front of a starving man, tell him not to eat anything, and then walk away for a few hours, it's pretty obvious what's going to happen. I swiped a Tiger Milk Bar out of the box without any of my peers or instructors finding out. Then I simply walked into a Porta-John and stuffed my face. I made sure there was no evidence. I rolled the wrapper up into my sleeve and popped a piece of chewing gum into my mouth (gum was allowed in limited quantity). I walked over to a trash bag when nobody was looking, and shoved the silvery wrapper into a grubby-looking MRE box until it was out of sight. I returned to my buddies with a semifull stomach. In my mind, I had done the right thing, and I had only capitalized on the mistakes of the instructors. I told absolutely nobody about this event.

They fed us a few hours later (another MRE) and allowed us an unprecedented six hours of sleep. This was unheard of at Sapper school. Part of the reason for the extended sleep time was that only half the platoon had fireguard, and I wasn't a part of the half that did. I lucked out. I awoke the next morning "refreshed" and ready.

The first few days in the field were "cadre-led patrolling." The absolute strangest thing about this training was that this was a concept I had developed on my own that I had tried to implement toward the end of my spring semester of my senior year in ROTC. My reasoning was that to teach someone how to lead effectively, they must be led by those who know how to execute a mission properly (in ROTC, the senior class). My plan didn't follow through that semester, but here it was integrated into the training. Essentially, we got to see "what right looked like," and I felt a bit vindicated that an idea I came up with was actually part of the US Army Sapper training. These missions contained an incredible amount of detail. You name it, it mattered—everything from a squad leader physically checking that each and every one of his soldiers had a round locked and loaded before stepping out on mission, down to making sure that the safety was on safe and not fire, down to making sure the machine gun was not a millimeter out of place in terms of deployment in a patrol base. The level of detail that was expected from us was absolutely amazing. As much as I "loved to hate" this aspect, I'm glad it was beaten into me. Even in the civilian world, I think differently now and always check everything before I go out somewhere (fluids in a car, writing utensils for class, and many other things that have become unconscious actions).

6/18
Didn't sleep at all last night. Worked through straight until 0600. Wet from dew.
Looked like it was about to rain…(couldn't finish)
Seven hours of sleep (two meals)

6/19
Day four of ten in the field. They have been overworking us, but so far we have been handling it well. Got seven hours of sleep last night, so I'm refreshed again (only because they screwed up fireguard). The weather has been perfect so far. Graded missions start today, and, honestly, I have no idea what I'm doing, so I hope I won't have to go first. The hand warmers I brought (that I caught hell for) come in good use. I pop one in my cap every morning. Gotta take care of myself…gotta just make it home…
1245 totally burned out. Lightheaded. Lack of motivation. Can't keep up with things. Wish I was reading this rather than writing it.
1545 broken
1700 have energy for some reason
Zero hours (two meals)

Dad had gotten me a large bag of hand warmers before leaving. On zero day, when we had the layout, the instructors had a field day when they saw them. They sneered at me in baby voices and asked if I didn't like the cold, et cetera. My peers jumped in too, some giving me an even harder time. I silently grinned through the ribbing until one of my classmates said, "If you really think you need hand warmers when we go to the field, you shouldn't be here." I just looked at him and said nothing.

In the field, I brought all the warmers I had. I gave most of them away. One day, that same classmate came up to me and, hat in hand, told me that he had heard I had extra warmers and asked if he could have one. I never took my eyes off him as I reached into my pocket and said, "If you really think you need a hand warmer, you shouldn't be here." He looked up, a trace of shock on his face. I smiled, laughed kiddingly, and said, "It's all good; here ya go, man." He thanked me and moved away.

6/20

Just got done with one of the most miserable days and nights I've ever had. Sergeant fucking [name removed] is such a dumbass fuckoff. He gave us three minutes to eat last night, that fat bastard. It rained all night, no sleep at all. And here we go with day five. Fuck that guy!

P.S. Connor's gone; we're down to thirty-eight. Out of gum; they didn't send me nearly enough. Rain is holding for now.

One and a half hours (one meal)

Consuming a meal at Sapper school is not what you might think. If a whole MRE could be consumed in the time allotted, it was a rare occasion. Typically when the meals were handed out, the routine was to eat as much as you could in five minutes, and then it would be straight back to training. A large trash bag came around, and whether you were finished or not with the meal, it all went in the bag. There was absolutely no saving food whatsoever. I got fairly adept at consuming most of an MRE in five minutes out of necessity. In the instance in this entry, the SI was upset with us for our "lack of motivation" that day and took away two minutes of chow time. This translated directly to food not consumed. Two minutes out of five meant that, at the very least, the loss of two-fifths of that meal. It was more than frustrating, and hence the tone in this entry.

Though I did not address it in my notes, about halfway through our field training, we were brought back to the base camp compound. As we marched in, we noticed a large pen with about twenty rabbits inside, and a large coop with about twenty chickens. We knew we were going to be fed soon, and I had heard rumors about this. This was the Sapper school "kill" class.

Our food was the chickens and rabbits. First, the instructors showed us the proper way to kill both the chicken and the rabbit. I knew what to do with the chicken, and it is fairly easy. Just pick one up by the neck and spin it around until it stops flapping. It's called wringing the neck. They also showed us how to hypnotize the chicken and then use the break in the middle of your combat boot to pop the head off.

The rabbit was a different story. One of our instructors picked a rabbit up by the hind legs and petted it gently for several minutes, stressing the fact that rabbits get scared easily. If they get too scared, the meat will sour and taste awful, he said. Once the rabbit was calm, he showed us how to find the nook in the back of the rabbit's head. After he showed us, using a quick karate chop, he hit it in the back of the head. Hitting it in that spot with enough force cleanly broke the neck, and he stated that it was very important that we do this correctly. The animal was giving its life for us so that we could eat, and he didn't want anyone to have to hit it more than twice.

Then they showed us how to skin both animals, which doesn't require a description. I would never have done this except I was so damn hungry. I put up with the blood, guts, and gore so that I could eat a square meal. It was still a bit nauseating cracking bones, cutting through tissue, and tearing off skin like wrapping paper. We were ordered to partner up and select either a rabbit or a chicken. I was the odd man out and had to select, kill, and clean an animal by myself.

Most of my buddies selected rabbits, and rushed to the rabbit pen once they were released. As they picked up the rabbits, the animals started freaking out and, almost in unison, started to *scream*. I had never known it was even possible for a rabbit to scream, let alone heard one do so. Amid the sounds of "Eeeeeeeee! Eeeeeeee! Eeeeeee!" you could hear the hard-packing sounds of karate chops. Some rabbits needed two hits—some even three. It was pretty rattling to me. I mean, I wanted to eat, but I didn't want my food to fight for its life, and I didn't want to watch as blood flew out of its nose (indicating the neck had been severed from the spine). Despite my hunger, I was still a bit wary about such things, so I grabbed a chicken. Killing it was no problem, but cleaning it was a bit…messy. I've cleaned birds before, but I've never skinned one, and—long story short—this thing took me about forty-five minutes to do by myself, and nearly killed my appetite.

We threw our meat in a Folgers coffee can with a handful of rice, a small potato, a carrot, and some canteen water. We let them sit on a fire for fifteen minutes, after which we were told the food was safe to eat. After mine was done, I took it over to a table, sat down, and sank my teeth into a piece of meat. It was as tough as rubber and tasted about the same. I spat it out, looked at my piece, and dropped it back in the bucket. I had quite a bit of rice, so I ate all of that first, then the potato, and then the carrot. Afterward, I called it a night. I maybe had a few bites of the chicken I had just killed, and threw out the rest. Thus ended the "kill" class.

Around this time, Kettinger, Darroch, and I were selected to be the machine gun team. In a machine gun team, one soldier is designated the gunner, one the assistant gunner, and one the ammo-bearer. We took pride in our work. We always drew an accurate range card, set up fire lanes, and ensured the tripod was adjusted to provide a final protective line (FPL). One night, in the pitch-dark Missouri woods, I became disoriented and couldn't find my team. I heard Darroch and Ket whisper loudly, "Voznick, over here!" I turned in time to see both through my night-vision goggles, reaching out to guide me to the fighting position. Due to the restrictive nature of the night-vision goggles we were using, neither was aware of the exact position of the other. Ket tripped over the gun and Darroch tripped over Ket. They both fell in a heap on the gun. I ran over to the barely moving mass of bodies. "Are you guys OK?" I exclaimed. Darroch rolled over, groaning, with a large gash on his nose. Kettinger sat up and looked dazed but unscathed. Darroch had not only cut himself, but must have suffered a mild concussion. He had hit his head and acted so strangely for the next hour or so that I became worried that it might be serious, even by Sapper school standard. He insisted that he would be OK, and fortunately by morning he seemed back to his old self.

Injuries at Sapper school were a common occurrence. We all had our own cuts, bruises, sprains, infections, sicknesses, and other assorted miseries that we all quietly endured. Up until this point, we had lost five of our number to broken bones or serious infections like cellulitis, a disgusting infection caused by the mixing of the sweat and grime we were constantly submerged in. I mention Connor at the end of this entry because Connor was the only one who *came back.*

The field was tougher on some than others, and Connor seemed to be one of the former. He seemed more worn down than most. Once, while on patrol, Connor left his weapon on "fire" instead of "safe." I witnessed one of the SIs pull his trigger when he left his weapon on the ground while taking some notes. For this, some of the soldiers in his chain of command were failed. The whole thing could have been forgiven, but instead of apologizing or hanging his head, Connor cried out, "But it was on safe!" When he left the field, it was because he had actually quit, which hadn't happened in our class yet. How the SIs allowed this was beyond me, but he departed the field with no obvious injury or infection. When Connor came back the next day, he acted energized and refreshed—nothing like the broken man from twenty-four hours earlier. He maintained this attitude all the way to graduation when he actually received his tab. There were quite a few of my peers who were more than upset by this.

6/21

Evening and night of June 20 was total hell. Rucked approximately eight miles just to go from patrol base to patrol base. We attempted to conduct missions, and they would yell at us and smoke us for anything they could afterward. The rucks were fast and brutal. Soaked my uniform with sweat. Feels like dirty cardboard. June 21 no better. Treat us shitty; feed us only once or twice a day if we're lucky. Tried to be PL (platoon leader) today. Felt terrible, performed terrible, and was fired. Failure feels awful, but the living conditions are far worse. I'm at a loss for words. I miss home.
Three hours (two meals)

I was "fired" as platoon leader because I did a crummy job. I did not know the "OPORD" format at all and, despite my warnings to all those in leadership, they allowed me to fail. I tried to tell them, "You guys, I really don't know how to do this. There are a lot of gaps here in my plan." The responses were, "Nah, you got this, Voznick. Just be confident." Confidence doesn't move a pencil on paper, and I had some serious flaws with the OPORD, but I presented as best I could—which was terribly. I didn't try to BS my way through any of it as some of my peers did. If I did not know the section or fully understand it, I skipped it. The OPORD I was supposed to deliver should have lasted upward of twenty minutes. I think it lasted all of two or three.

When I was finished, the SIs brought in the entire platoon, something that had never been done before. For better or for worse, I always seemed to stand out. I was never just another face in the crowd. That time it was for worse. Though the SIs acknowledged that I lacked a lot of knowledge, they flew into the rest of our leadership for "failing the PL." The SIs had noted that I had tried to get some help from some of the more knowledgeable folks in our group but since they had not helped, the entire chain of command was failed. I only had a problem with that last part. Because of me, my team had received "No Gos"—at least that was the way I saw it, even if the SIs didn't. I felt I had screwed over my buddies and violated one of my cardinal rules. One of the graders was SSG Harding. After all was said and done, I approached him and insisted that it was my failure and not my peers' that was the cause of the poor performance. He had none of it, and the decision stood. I was pretty quiet for a few hours after that one, but we all got over it by the end of the day, and things returned to normal.

The smoke sessions were a regular occurrence. At the conclusion of *every* mission, we were punished for not being able to account for our equipment in a "timely" manner, and they really tore into us for the smallest problem. They would always yell out during our agony, "You know why we're doing this to you? You know why we're not feeding you and not letting you sleep? You know why we're smoking you? It's because *shithead* down range doesn't care about you. *Shithead* wants you tired and wants you hungry. *Shithead* don't give a *fuck about you*! *And neither do we*!" We were reminded repeatedly of this particular fact. It had a way of making me more conscious of where I stepped, lest I fall and sprain an ankle. It made me more conscious of how I packed my ruck, so certain tools would be more accessible in a shorter amount of time. It made me more aware of my situation in general. *Nobody is going to look out for you. You're on your own; take care of yourself. Even if you're dog tired and out of energy.*

6/22

Sixty-eight years ago, the Germans invaded Russia on this date. Past couple of years, I would tell Johnny that. We would be working and I would make him guess the significance. Hope all is well and good in Chino. Really want all things to be unchanged and happy when I get there. As soon as I get back I will have the parents standing by with ingredients to make a root beer float. Also have some A&W candies ready. Before I leave for San Diego on Sunday, I will eat a large egg/bacon/pancake b-fast. I will then have In-N-Out Burger @ SD for lunch. Probably Islands for dinner.

Day Seven and obviously all thoughts are on one thing. The barracks will be a nice transition instead of coming straight home. I can at least get a jump-start on fattening myself back up.

At its worst, it's the feeling of being sick with a cold and hung over at the same time. Then I'm usually asked to carry a hundred-pound ruck and run a few miles. It wouldn't be so bad except that we get only two meals a day…sometimes only one. We also sleep about an hour and a half every two days. Surprisingly, the human body is able to withstand the punishment. There is a lot more I could say about the misery, but it wouldn't be fun to imagine, so maybe I'll tell some more stuff later. Day five was so far my worst day, but I think I have gotten used to things a bit. We're all thinning out a bit, so I won't look very good for a while. But in the few minutes of "free time," we all talk about what we're going to eat when we get out…and it's a lot of food we plan on eating, so we will fatten up. As soon as I get to the airport, I'm going to have a bloody Mary, and as soon as I get to Chino, I'm going to have an A&W root beer float. Don't ask me why, I just want one. Can't wait to get back and do everything that I took for granted. The desert, dirt bikes, and music are my favorite things to think about. I hope I snap back fast to the easy summer life when I get back. I want to purge my memory of…this. One hour (one meal)

The music I would sometimes hum to myself, but I had a particular song that I would sing that I could always get a few of the guys to sing as well. I would begin either on a patrol through the woods or when we were deploying our perimeter. It's easiest to imagine this as the scene in *Forrest Gump*; that's what inspired me, anyway—a bunch of dirty-looking soldiers in a formation marching through thick woods/jungle. "There's something happening here. / What it is ain't exactly clear." I would sing while bobbing my head to get the beat right. "There's a man with a gun over there," I would point in any direction, "ahh telling me I got to beware." Others near me would pick up the chorus: "Stop, children, what's that sound? / Everybody look what's going down…" Knowing the whole song, I would fill in all the verses, and my buddies would help out with the chorus. The verses always came out mixed up, and we never did finish a whole song. Sleep and food deprivation have a way of making simple things like this difficult. But in terms of keeping a sense of humor, this was one of the ways I stayed in the game, and my friends, who had already labeled me as the funny kid from California, seemed to enjoy it. There was a mix of others I would hum, including Scott McKenzie's "If You're Going to San Francisco," and Gentry would sometimes spin up "Pour Some Sugar on Me" by Def Leppard.

A typical conversation we had originated around this time: "How ya holdin' up, Voznick?" Olson asked while we were sitting on the perimeter one day.

"Man, ya know, I could be on a beach in California right now. Or racing my dirt bike. But no, I'm good, really I am. I'm glad to have the shit kicked outta me. I like getting sleep deprived and starved. I liked having my ass sent halfway across the states to this shithole with all you shitbags…like you, Ket." (This was all in good fun.) "'You'll be a Sapper, Voznick! That's badass!' they told me. 'OK,' I said. 'Anything I need to know?' 'Nah, it'll suck, but you'll be fine.'" I looked over at Kettinger after my little play and said, "I dunno, Ket, whaddya think? Because I think we're fuckin' loony to volunteer for shit like this."

Olson and Kettinger were laughing quietly. Kettinger spoke up, "Doesn't make much sense, does it? It must sure be a far cry from California."

The final paragraph in this entry is fairly straightforward. The misery is pretty well described. Another aspect of the misery is that of the insects. I have been in the field with the bugs before, but this was something else. It was on a *regular basis* that one would feel ticks crawling up and down one's legs.

During Sapper time, a brief half hour or so in the mornings, we were allowed to change and conduct hygiene, and there were always at least a couple ticks that we had to pull off of our bodies. Deer ticks were the primary type. They would weasel in, usually around my waistline, and bite. Contrary to what I had been taught in the Boy Scouts, simply pulling the little bastards off your skin sufficed for their extermination. On one occasion, I had a rather large tick bite the back of my leg. I had a buddy take that one out, and he twisted it off. He said that by twisting it, the jaws wouldn't stay in, which I immediately dismissed as another bullshit remedy. (Another one I heard is to eat match heads. If you believe any of this, save yourself the trouble of talking about it with me because I think anyone who believes this crap is a superstitious witch doctor.) That tick left a mark on my skin that was visible for five months after the course.

Fortunately, by the time the ticks became a real problem, we were destroyed in every sense of the word, and so when we finally sat down to rest or sleep, the itsy bitsy crawling of the ticks going up our legs didn't bother us in the least. One of the instructors had even said that if we felt the ticks, "Let them eat," and so we did. (No, it was virtually impossible to kill the ticks through our pant legs—have you ever tried to kill one with your hands? They don't die easily.)

It's also clear that around this time, day sixish, my mental state started to waver. Cravings for foods or drinks were common. Dementia was just around the corner.

"I want to purge my memory of…this." At that time, I was extremely fearful of becoming a different person entirely. Though I don't consider myself to be an overly religious person, I felt very desperate and found myself clasping my hands together and praying silently from time to time. I begged God not to let this place change me. I felt that I would never be the same again, and it terrified me more than my worst nightmare. In the state of mind I was in, I truly felt it wasn't too much to ask. Every passing day, however, I could almost feel the essence of my character slipping ever so slowly away.

6/23

I'm just starting to smell the finish line. We started patrolling, and it is tough. The standard yesterday and for the next two days is one meal a day and one hour of sleep in the early morning. This amounts to just over two hours of "free time" for every twenty-two hours of patrolling. It's not been too bad, though. We pull security and talk about freedoms and foods we are going to enjoy as soon as we get back to civilization. I'm still sticking to my bloody-Mary-sleep-on-the-plane-eat-A&W-in-Chino plan as my first course of action. Tomorrow is day nine, and the last full day. Still it is no easy task; a six-mile ruck march is due this evening.

On the twenty-third, I tried dip for the first time (and last). Everyone was doing it, and it looked like it helped my buddies stay alert. I was ready to try anything to take my mind off the misery. Olson gave me a pinch of his Copenhagen. I placed it between my lip and gums and went into the prone position. Almost immediately I got a buzz from the nicotine. Having never really experienced any tobacco products, and lacking food and sleep, I went into a drunken stupor. I tried to man up and handle it at first, but once I felt as if I was spinning in circles, I spit out the pinch. "What the fuck, dude?" I said aloud. I tried to stand up, and suddenly my rifle felt ten times heavier. "Shit…" I flopped back down.

"Hey, Voznick, you all right?" Olson asked, laughing.

"No I'm not all right. If we move out right now, I'll barely be able to stand." Olson continued to laugh. "Laugh it up, ass. Seriously, what do I do?"

"Just stand up and take a walk around the perimeter. Make it look like you're checking on everyone and making sure they're awake."

I took his advice, and, after two or three stumbling, slow-motion walks around the security perimeter, I finally felt well enough to sit back down. The platoon moved out shortly thereafter. Had the instructors decided it was my turn to be in a leadership rotation, I would have been completely ineffective. Fortunately, I was not selected, and the buzz slowly wore off…slowly. I have not done dip since then and don't plan on doing it again.

6/24

The six-miler hurt a lot, but on the ninth, I was made SL (squad leader). This was good because it was an easy way to get a "Go" as opposed to PL (platoon leader), or PSG (platoon sergeant). Bailey was my PL in the morning and delivered a terrible OPORD, but we got moving. My ruck's left arm strap broke off, and I thought I was done for, but Ket is proficient at knots. Rucked about eight miles.

The first sentence in this entry is referring to a ruck march that we had to do the evening of the twenty-third. To describe it, I used the words "hurt a lot," and I'll take a moment to describe what "hurt a lot" means here.

This march took place on a hardball (asphalt) road. The instructors kept us at a jogging pace (keep in mind that at the lightest, our rucks' weight at any given time was *at least* seventy to eighty pounds). In addition to the weight of my ruck, I was put in charge of the M240 for the march. We had to keep a belt of about sixty rounds locked and loaded in case we made contact and needed suppression fire. Keeping the machine gun at about hip height, the belt dangles nearly to the ground, and so I wrapped the belt around the gun itself. After about a mile or so, I began falling back. Despite being better acclimated and more adept in the ways of Sapper school, I still had trouble keeping up with so much weight. At about two miles in, Gentry, a southerner, someone I barely had any contact with, came running to the rear of the formation. "Hey, Voznick!" he said with a grin. "How ya doing back here?" I didn't say anything, even after he started humming some of the Sapper cadences. "Well, Voznick, how 'bout we switch weapons for a bit, whaddya say?"

Of the men and women who protect this country while you sleep or as you go about your day, I'm convinced that some of the best were at this school. Here we were, exhausted, starved, yelled at, and punished, and this guy wanted to take the machine gun from me. He did not have to. He had hauled it earlier and done his time. I was trailing the formation and would likely suffer a bad smoking, and this kid from the South whom I barely knew actually *wanted* to help me. I reluctantly accepted and immediately felt better with an M16 in my hands. At about mile four or five, the sun was completely down. Then, with the entire platoon stretched out along about a quarter mile of highway, the "enemy" decided to engage.

When looking through NVGs (night-vision goggles), everything looks like a dream—or a nightmare from some crappy scary movie. The action opened with arty simulators. As I crashed to the ground and hurried to unhook my ruck, I saw flashes from the tree line on one side of the road. I was at the front of the formation when the fighting started. Gentry was still toward the rear, where the fighting was breaking out. That was when I heard and saw Gentry's 240. While watching down the road, I could see the small, lighted pops of small arms from the tree line and the same lighted popping of our return fire. The roar of the 240 and the light it created was significant, and the staccato of my sixty-round belt filled the air for several minutes and then fell silent. Gentry was out of ammo. Most of the rest of it was inside the ruck I was carrying. After about an hour of a confused melee, the leadership finally brought order, and we started moving out. The "wounded" were gathered up along with their gear (another seventy or eighty pounds we had to drag).

We moved up the road another mile or so before the instructors finally told us to stop and reform. We complied. We were dripping with sweat (and I mean our entire uniforms were drenched as if we had been in a shower), exhausted, and quite miserable, and so the instructors decided to PT us. We had to take our rucks, put them above our heads, and conduct presses. If we hit our heads or dropped our rucks, instructors would make our lives even more miserable. This went on for about twenty minutes or so before we were finally allowed to move out to our patrol base for the evening.

I got in touch with Gentry somewhere in there and apologized for not being with him during the fight. He replied, still smiling, "Ah, no problem, I just wish there had been a bit more ammo!" And so "hurt a lot" was the best way I could describe this rather typical incident at Sapper school. It was, and continues to be as I write this, more than mildly frustrating that words cannot fully describe these situations. To fully appreciate them, they must simply be experienced.

The twenty-fourth. This day was by far the most "stoically dramatic." Things happened that would have been "game over" in any regular training exercise with a regular unit, but here, *serious* injury and *serious* infection were the only ways out. Bailey (my old land navigation buddy) kicked off the morning with an OPORD that was about as good as mine had been. After that screw-up, we moved out on our mission, which involved surmounting an obstacle: a cliff. This just so happened to be the exact same cliff we had practiced on about a week earlier. On the way, my ruck broke. When it happened, I was astonished. I stared at the dangling arm strap and quickly realized the damage was permanent. The support button on my strap had turquoise-blue corrosion caked on it. This button was tucked away, and I hadn't known it even existed until then. This particular ruck was from the ROTC stock. My personal ruck (one that I used my own money to buy because I did not trust ROTC equipment) was too small for Sapper school, and so I had to borrow this one from our supply. *Bullshit!* I thought. I could not physically carry my load without the strap. CPT Simpson happened to be nearby, and he had seen my predicament. "Sir," I asked incredulously, "what should I do?"

Though CPT Simpson was the only SI who was also an officer, this did not equate to a softer touch. CPT Simpson was perhaps the most intense of the SIs, and so this was not a wise thing for me to address him over. Fortunately, he simply sat and stared at me through his sunglasses and said nothing. Within a second I understood that there was no help or sympathy coming from the instructors—of course I knew that by now. I moved to the front of the formation and found Kettinger. I really had no idea what was going to happen now. Then Ket saved my ass. With the whole platoon grounded because of my problem, many peered in to watch as SGT Kettinger quickly and expertly tied a series of knots using 550 cord. When he was done, the pack was fully adjustable, and we were able to continue our mission, to my total relief. That had truly been the closest of calls. I told Kettinger that I owed him a beer for that one.

When we reached the cliff, we had to go over with all the equipment we had on us, so we jumped with upwards of eighty pounds attached to us. Almost all of us "opossumed," or ended up going down the cliff upside down. As I locked myself in, I slipped as I tried to lower myself down on the bars, and I immediately opossumed. Of course nothing can just be ordinary with me. For such a rappel, we had to use a special tool to hook ourselves in. It looked like a big silver lima bean, and mine caught on one of the large metal bars. Without going into detail, this tightened my Swiss seat to a dangerous point. It essentially turned me into a nut inside a nutcracker. I was upside down, having the life squeezed out of me. Very quickly everything became dark, and through the blackening void (what I imagine was blood not getting to my head) I could hear the instructors screaming. "*Voznick*, hit your carabiner! *Hit it as hard as you can and keep hitting it!*" I don't remember how many times I ended up hitting it—maybe two or three—but the vibrations finally popped the lima bean over the bar, and I free fell about eighty feet. It would have been the end of me, but my good buddy Darroch was on the belay and kept me from serious harm. I lay in a heap on the ground in utter pain. Darroch and someone else helped me up and got me to where the platoon was deployed.

It was my kidneys—at least that was what it felt like. Sharp, *really sharp*, pains permeated my insides for the next several hours. My bladder felt terrible, and I was convinced I was going to pee blood. Even though I was barely able to move, I whipped it out where I lay and peed. No blood. Nothing. By Sapper school standards, I was OK, and a little bitch if I said otherwise. I would carry on. Again. *It could always be worse…right?*

As soon as the rest of the platoon was over the cliff, we formed up and moved out. The next obstacle, still on the same mission, was a river. We approached the river tactically. We had been trained to deploy a rope bridge and cross, but the water level didn't look too deep. The big ropes were brought forward, and those of us in the leadership, including Kettinger—who was PSG and fast becoming a good friend of mine—had a quick discussion.

"Forget the rope," I said. "We're gonna take too much time setting it up, and they'll start throwing arty sims. I say we just ford it."

"You think we can ford it, Voznick?" Ket asked.

"Absolutely. Setting up a bridge will take way too much time. We'll probably do a shitty job setting it up, and it's completely unnecessary."

One or two of the other squad leaders objected, saying something to the effect of, "I would set up the bridge because I think that's what we're supposed to do." It was nonsense that would lead to bad times and embarrassment. Thankfully, after the brief discussion, Kettinger made the decision: no bridge! Ket had approved the plan but specifically wanted my squad and me to cross first. I brought my squad forward, informed them of what was happening, turned to the river, and then said, "OK, let's go." I took point and led my squad across while the rest of the platoon spread out on the river's edge covering us. My job was to get across as quickly as possible and set up a rally point (RP) so the rest of our platoon could form up correctly on the opposite bank.

Robotically, I moved across. One deep spot almost went above my chest, but it was nothing serious. As soon as I made it to the other side, I motioned to Kettinger that the stream was indeed fordable. The rest of my squad was now about halfway across. I scaled an embankment and turned around just in time to see several large geysers burst from the river. Those who were in the water let out grunts and groans as the shock from the arty sims impacted on them. Suddenly, everyone began yelling, *"Hurry up! Let's go! Move it, move it!"* For the few seconds I turned to watch. The Sapper instructors were laughing and throwing arty sims (a small, loud explosive used in training to simulate indirect fire) into the water, some landing only a few feet away from my squad mates. I moved on and selected an RP. Once the rest of us had crossed the river, we took accountability and moved out.

We marched for a few miles through terrain that looked like a jungle straight out of Vietnam. There were no trails, and we had to make our own. Fortunately, my squad was not the point squad, and thus we crept along through grass that was five to six feet high. The humidity was sweltering, and to top it off, we were thoroughly soaked either by sweat or river water or both. Misery. But the job came first, and the misery took a backseat. We plodded on, and, finally, the jungle-type stuff ended—and was replaced by a steep incline. This miserable situation went on and on for hours until the platoon went black (ran out) of water. By the time that happened, we were almost done with the mission, and so our instructors pushed us to the end.

Once the mission had been completed, the SIs made a big fuss about how it was our fault for going black on water. They had no sympathy, and we did not refill our canteens until we got to our next patrol base, which was about a four-mile march down the road. I had never been so thirsty, but by then I was used to the fact and understood that the Sapper school instructors really did not care about us in the conventional sense. I wouldn't go as far as to call them tab protectors, but they knew full well that the human body could be pushed beyond breaking point after breaking point and still function—and they had no problem breaking us down like that.

We formed up in the new patrol base and changed leadership. Though used to a large amount of misery by then, most of us were taking issue with the sweat/river water mixture that drenched us. It was causing many of us particular agony, and as soon as the new leadership rotated (the PL and PSG), I requested that the men rotate off the line to change their boots and socks. Surprisingly, our new PL granted the request. I didn't wait around for him to change his mind and immediately had half of my squad pull off the line and change. As soon as they were done, I rotated the other half and myself. We did this in the pitch dark of night. Without night vision goggles, we could not see our hands in front of our faces. It was like being trapped in a cave: total blackness. The NVGs we used were a monocular type that fit on a Kevlar helmet. Doing something simple like changing your boots and socks in an environment like this was time consuming. In all seriousness, it took a full forty-five minutes for my squad to change their socks. The other SLs had hesitated to give the order and wanted instead to maintain a state of complete "readiness," but I wasted no time in my decision. After all, the only thing I was concerned about was the health and welfare of my buddies—not the tab. Perhaps the others were worried about losing their tab?

When we finally moved out, my squad was the only one with warm, dry feet. One of my proudest moments at Sapper school came the following morning, the last day of Sapper school. Some guys in another squad were complaining about their feet being wet from the previous day. They talked to some of the guys in my squad and were surprised when they heard, "No, my feet are dry. Our squad leader had us change out last night. Yours didn't?"

To top off that night, a fire ant bit me. I had never been bitten by a fire ant, and when I felt a large insect crawl across the back of my neck, I swatted at it, thinking it was a spider. As I did, I felt a large stinging sensation. I happened to be giving orders at the time and let out an agonized groan. "What happened?" asked one of my team leaders.

"Shit, I just got bitten by a spider." I finished giving the orders through the stinging pain. The SIs had been very stern about spider bites in the woods. They were no joke. I thought for a moment. *I was just bitten by a spider…and they told us if that ever happened, to call the medics. The only spiders that bite out here are black widows and brown recluses. But I don't want to cry wolf and be hounded down by the SIs. Who knows what they would do to me?* I found Hubbard (I called him L. Ron) who had some medical experience and described what happened. He flat-out told me to go to the medics and not to screw around about it. Long story short, the SIs actually showed a lot of concern and brought out a medic who diagnosed me. I went back to the line just in time to complete the mission. We moved out to our last patrol base at around 0100, and I was relieved of my duties. My grade would be given to me the following day.

6/25
(No entry)

After the one hour of sleep on the night of day seven, we were not allowed to nap again, and received only one meal a day in the morning until we were out of the field. This was the long haul. On the last morning, I experienced a small amount of delirium. Yanak was with me in our fighting position. The dawn was just barely beginning to rise on the last official day of Sapper school. A small amount of light shone through the trees, and suddenly I was staring at the bombed-out ruins of several five-story buildings. My mind was slow to react (literally). What I was seeing was similar to an optical illusion. The skyline had come forward and the tree line had moved back. My depth perception was whack, and so the outline of the dawn between the trees appeared to be ruined buildings. I subconsciously figured this out and just kind of enjoyed the show. "Dude. Yanak, I'm finally hallucinating. I see burned-out buildings."

Yanak slowly nodded his head. He was suffering from fatigue and was barely able to stay awake. "Hah, I'm tripping balls, dude," I laughed. Yanak didn't say anything.

At that point in the training, we were no longer allowed to pull security by lying prone on the ground. The SIs knew that we would literally pass out from exhaustion if allowed to lie prone. In order to stay awake, we were ordered to stand up, and Yanak finally crashed. Funny thing, it's actually possible to fall asleep while you stand. But typically you'll wake up when your knees collapse, and you can catch yourself. Yanak unfortunately didn't wake up. First, his rifle dropped out of his hands and landed on the ground in front of him. He started to keel over. Then he fell down with a loud thud as he smacked into the ground and on top of his rifle. It might sound funny, but actually, it's pretty dangerous. Imagine standing up straight. Tie your arms behind your back and then force yourself to fall forward. The potential for injury is significant, and I quickly helped him back up. He was a bit bruised, but otherwise OK. The instructors were laughing.

I received my evaluation for squad leader and, to my surprise, I received a "Go." My grader's reasoning was that I performed satisfactorily on all counts, but it was with dissemination of information that I really shined. ROTC gets some credit here. They taught us that the squad leader should never be sitting still. The catch is that although I agree with this, it is sometimes difficult in a twenty-four-hour operating period to be constantly checking—or pretending to check—on your squad. I made up a few of my own rules. If in perimeter, I would move around tactically and lie in the prone with individual fighting positions. I always started out with the basics: make sure weapons are on safe, ensure full magazines, properly set up machine gun, lock in fields of fire. I had no idea who my grader was and I didn't care (so I wasn't putting on a show). I was doing this stuff to help my squad, not myself. After taking care of business and sometimes making a joke out of it, I would shoot the shit for a couple minutes with whomever I was with. I would always ask where he or she was from and other bullshit questions, but my favorite was, "So what are you good at? What's your talent?" The answers were always worth a good conversation.

But always, *always*, I would find out as much information about the mission as I could and let them know. I would let them know things they would actually care about: obstacles, distance, terrain type en route, approximate hit times, next chow, next sleep, et cetera. I would try to put things in a positive spin but was sincere, and I was always joking about our situation. I did these things because nobody else ever let me really know what was going on with the mission until we were moving out, and I didn't like that. Once we were on mission, I would move up through the squad at any halt and make sure they were all there and ask them if they needed anything. I would also try to find out what the holdups were, and then of course I would let my squad know everything I found out. Knowledge is power.

We moved out on our last mission, which was a bunker complex assault. I haven't explained any of our missions because they were all pretty much the same and wouldn't be worth writing down, but this one deserves some detail. We moved out in squad wedges and made it to the objective rally point (ORP) in good order. We were ordered to do a preliminary assault on the bunkers, which were surrounded by protective concertina wire. A few of our guys needed to place and prime a Bangalore torpedo to clear the wire from our path, and our attack was to ensure this got done properly. A Bangalore is a large explosive that typically looks like a long piece of pipe. It's used to breach obstacles (in *Saving Private Ryan*, they use one in the beginning of the movie).

As we assaulted, I noticed there were four or five rows of barbed wire between the bunkers and us. The machine gun fire from the bunkers was loud and continuous. The torpedo was placed, and we pulled back and waited inside special bunkers for the explosion. In by far the largest amount of explosive power I've felt or witnessed, the torpedo exploded and threw a column of dirt into the air. When we were finally allowed to make our final assault, dust and bits of dirt were still falling through the air. We assaulted through and around the large gap where the wire used to be and made it into the enemy trenches. We suffered more casualties than I could recall on any other mission, but I guess that figures. The whole thing looked like a re-creation of a scene from *Saving Private Ryan*.

At the conclusion of the mission, one of the SIs yelled out, "All right, we've completed all the training. You're done with Sapper school!" Everyone, even though we were now at the verge of collapsing from exhaustion, let out a wild, exuberant cheer.

We weren't quite free though, not yet. We had to go back to our base camp and help clean up the gear. Once we were done with this, the SIs barbecued hot dogs. We all got two hot dogs and two Shasta colas. I sat down next to Kettinger and Darroch and slowly chewed my food. *Real food.* It had been weeks since I had eaten real food like this. I sat there and stared up into the sky. It was a feeling of total relaxation. The small dose of freedom was a shock to my system, and I savored this very surreal moment. My bubble burst when one of the SIs smoked us strictly because he said he wanted to get one more in before we were released—the bastard. We were smoked and then taken back to barracks. It was all over—or so it seemed.

CHAPTER SIX

Retest

*"I finished thirteen miles of a twelve-mile course with the 'runs' and no
underwear. I took a test on demolitions calculations while listening to
an imaginary woman and her baby crying outside the room."*

This was the most epic finale that I could have experienced. A feeling of
elation swept over me when the instructors exclaimed, "You're done with
Sapper school!" on our last mission. Had I known what was about to happen,
I wouldn't have had such a warm feeling. Writing this last part, it seems almost
made up. But all of this actually happened. At the end of June in 2008, I finished Sapper school. Some of this is hard even for me to believe, but there were
witnesses to prove all of it—albeit shocked witnesses.

Upon arriving back at barracks, they split us into two groups. The group
I was in was nineteen strong (the original class size was forty-five). At that
point I had checked out mentally and was simply counting the hours until I
would be on a plane home. I had long ago given up on the tab. (I had never
given up on myself or my buddies, which may have been the root cause for my
eventual success.) One of the instructors approached as I was daydreaming.
"Congratulations," he said flatly. "You all qualify to pass the Sapper Leader
Course." I was stunned. Then he broke into a smile. "Some of you, however,
need to take a few makeup tests." As he read off the names, he got to mine and
stated, "Voznick: twelve-mile foot march and demolitions test."

Sapper school has three major areas that require at least a grade of 70 percent to pass (aside from the field exercises): the land navigation course, the twelve-mile march, and the demolitions calculations test. The nineteen of us had enough points to pass Sapper school, but I personally had not scored 70 percent or better on the march or the demo test. The foot march I've explained. When I took the demo test, I had a fever and was sick with the flu. Of course, that is certainly not anything that could delay a test at Sapper school, and so I did the best I could and scored poorly. (Interestingly, I went through all the symptoms of a common cold in about fourteen hours, including a fever. I believe this is because of the state our bodies were in.)

How the hell did I qualify for this? I felt shocked and excited with a touch of disappointment. My disappointment stemmed from the fact that I knew what was going to happen. While my peers slept in tomorrow morning, I would be awake and forced to complete a twelve-mile foot march with forty pounds of weight in three hours. After just getting out of the field, this would be no easy task. The start time was 0400. To make matters worse, I had the demolitions test at 0900, and after the ten days in the field, I had "brain dumped" everything about demolitions. After we were released, I hurried over to the barracks and immediately started preparing. I had to borrow a ruck from one of my peers (mine had broken apart in the field), pack it, weigh it, and size it. This took about two or three hours. It was starting to get late when I finally started studying the demolitions calculations, and, as I tried to work through some sample problems, I realized I was doomed to failure. I had been up for well over forty-eight hours and eaten about two meals in that time. I could not focus. I was finished. *Well, whatever. I'll saddle up anyway.*

That was when Dues, the captain that I had encountered on my failed foot march at the beginning of Sapper school, rescued me. "Hey, Voz, congratulations. I hear you're in line for a tab," she said as she walked past my bunk.

"Yeah, but no, I'm not going to get it. I can't remember how to do this shit, and I'm really starting to pass out here." I couldn't have cared less, but she stopped in her tracks.

I won't ever forget the look of concern that showed on her face. "What do you need? We can help you. *You're gonna get that tab, Voznick,*" she said sternly. Those words again. Said differently and coming from CPT Dues, they practically rang in my ears. After talking briefly, we came up with a plan. She and another one of my buddies, Gierling, would stay up late and build up my note card (which was allowed on the test). This is how CPT Dues got me my Sapper tab. If there is one thing that I really regret after coming away from that school, it's the fact that I never thanked her for her help after all was said and done. Things moved very quickly, and I simply missed the opportunity.

For my part, I went outside and ordered some pizza and Nestea drinks because I figured I'd need some carbs for the next day's run. I wolfed down half the pizza and the two drinks in less than five minutes. I took a shower (*wow, a shower!*), called Dad and let him know what was happening, and then racked out. What I didn't know but would soon find out was that the pizza nearly undid all that I had accomplished.

I slept for what amounted to about an hour. In fact, I slept through my alarm. Fortunately, one of my buddies woke me up. I can't remember who. I think it was Gaylick. As I rucked up and prepared to move out, I looked around the barracks. About one in four of our crew was sitting or standing near his or her bunk. "Yanak, what the fuck are you doing?" I asked on my way out.

"Huh? Oh, I was...I..." He looked very confused. "I was checking to make sure all weapons have a round chambered. We're moving out soon."

"Yanak, you're freakin' out, man. We're not on the line anymore. Go back to sleep," I said. I started to walk out and noticed Tully doing the same thing. This was the state of our being. We were not used to sleeping, so used to the field, and so exhausted that we were having trouble adjusting to racking out in an actual bed for more than an hour. Some sat on their beds. Some were standing straight up, just sweating and babbling, talking to people who weren't there. It was eerie.

There were about five of us in the retest of the foot march. I didn't think that completing the march was possible because I was so broken physically and mentally. However, as I started running, I realized how much lighter my pack felt. I was used to carrying over eighty pounds of equipment, but with forty on my back, I felt like a feather. I ran forever. I ran like Forrest Gump. I didn't stop. I had once again snuck a few treats into my pockets in case I needed some energy. I made it to the eighth mile within an hour and forty-five minutes. I felt great, like a jackrabbit.

Rain clouds suddenly came out of nowhere, and a torrential rain came pouring down. I splashed and plodded along, staring straight at the ground in front of me. I was soaked in minutes, but I wasn't fazed in the least. Rainwater poured off my face as lightning started to flash all about me and thunder boomed louder than some of our explosives did. I just gritted my teeth, laughed out loud, and thought, *Somebody take a bloody picture! Make it one of those motivational posters.*

P-E-R-S-E-V-E-R-A-N-C-E.

At that moment, there was no man more fearless, lethal, confident, or undefeatable than Ryan Andrew Voznick. And I knew it…

Then my stomach started to rumble. After about five or ten minutes, I knew what was going on in there. My body was not taking the pizza/Nestea combo very well. It was dumb of me to think that I could just go back to eating normal food like that, but I had and there was no going back now. I tried my best to hammer on and ignore it. I had an experience like this at airborne school, where I nearly shit my pants while sitting in the parachute hanger with a full pack and chute on. *I can handle this, no problem.* The pressure built up. I knew I was going to explode if I didn't do something.

Finally, I reached a point where every nerve and every ounce of energy I had was being spent on trying *not* to shit my pants. I didn't know what else to do. I hooked right off the road and went in about ten feet. A Humvee would plod along every few minutes, and I just kept my fingers crossed that no more would come by. I threw my pack off my back and dropped my pants in two seconds flat. I squatted over the tall grass and shit a storm. I shat and shat, and then I shat again. For about five minutes, I gave it my all.

Toilet paper!

What the hell was I going to use to wipe my ass? This was far messier than I thought, and I wasn't about to just pull up my pants and run onward with all that disgust. I stared at my boxers. Nobody in the army ever wears boxers during training, which I think is disgusting. In a flash I ripped them in two (no, I did not slip them off—there was no way), and in two wipes, it was done. As I ran off, I glanced back and stared at my torn boxers lying in the sick. *That looks just…wrong.* I thought about who might find this scene.

I moved out back to the road and started running full steam. Then, right on the last mile stretch or so, I got lost. How this happened, I don't know. Maybe it was fatigue, or the fact that I had never seen the course in its entirety—but anyway, I got lost. I didn't realize that I was lost until I ended up on a hardball road. There weren't any hardballs on the correct route; I knew that for sure. I stopped running and started walking down the road in a random direction. I passed a private and stopped her. "Excuse me?" I asked as politely as I could. "Do you know where the Sapper training area is?" I said all this in a tone not unlike one a tourist would use when asking how to get back to his hotel. She had a look on her face as if she had just seen a ghost, or thought I was going to assault her or something. She just pointed down the road in the direction I was going, and I gave her a big smile and a "thank you!" With that, I heaved to and ran for the life of me.

The instructors and my buddies were all at the finish line, looking down the road trying to figure out where I was, when I came running down the back way. Baker saw me first and started yelling at the top of his lungs: "Voznick! *Get over here…now!* You've got one minute!" My veins pumped acid as I crossed the finish line, panting and sucking in air as if there was none left in the world. I was in such a sorry state at this point. I was soaked from head to foot in sweat, my stomach hurt, and my feet felt like they were bleeding, as if they had been rubbed off. I barely noticed that there was an incredible amount of laughter going on around me. The medics would soon tell me, and through it all, I slowly figured it out. Apparently, I, Ryan Voznick, am the only solider who has finished the foot march at Sapper school by crossing the finish line…from the opposite direction.

This was something not to be taken lightly, but for me there was still more shitting to be done, and that was my only concern. I was going to ask Baker for his drawers if he had any (yeah, no joke), but before I did, I spotted a roll of toilet paper in one of the Humvees. The medics said I could use it, and so I grabbed it, ran off into the woods a way, and relieved myself once again. After this, we were all helped into the Humvee and driven back to the barracks. There was continuous laughter and amazement on my behalf. The medics couldn't get over it. "Voznick, that was a whole extra mile you did, and you still made it in time, with the runs and all! That's amazing! After coming outta the field and all. You're fuckin' tough!"

I heard these things, but my mind was elsewhere. On any other day, I would have taken joy in playing it up and joking about it with them, but not now. I was so utterly broken, so bruised and beaten, so tired that I simply stared at the ground or just looked away. *What's the point in talking about it? Let's just get this over with.* Hearing everybody pay me all those compliments felt as if somebody was telling me my hair is brown. *Of course I'm tough. What on earth else would you call what just happened?* When they dropped us off at the barracks, I stepped down onto the pavement—and into a universe of total *pain*.

Ahhhhhhhgggggghhhh! I screamed in my head and closed my eyes.

Titanic waves of pain shot through my left nut all the way to my stomach, of all places. I could hardly walk! I collapsed where I stood, and somebody helped me up. I guess I ran myself so hard that my ball-crushing injury came back in all its glory. I grimaced and clenched my teeth but made no noise. *Damn, Ramirez!* I hobbled on (in fact, it was up through graduation day that I had a limp, which made it *physically impossible* to run and tough as hell just to walk). I walked inside the barracks and there, sitting nicely on my bunk, was my notecard in Dues's handwriting. In dark, black letters, she had written "Sapper Voznick" on my handbook. I showered, studied, and, before I knew it, 0900 was upon me. *One more test, one more hurdle, then it's all over. Whatever the outcome, it will be over...*

The test was fifty questions, and I could miss fifteen and still pass. I began after a brief review session with an SI. As the test progressed, I felt more and more woozy, more sleepy. I had been awake now for about seventy-two hours (excluding the hour or so power nap), and for the week before that, I had already been sleep deprived. Add to that the fact that we were burning far more calories than we were receiving and, yeah, I finally had a legitimate hallucination, and of course it had to be while I was taking my final test.

It went like this: I was trying to concentrate on my test problem when I heard pounding on the barracks door. The instructor was the only one in the room, but when I looked up he was gone. The pounding continued, and I heard a woman cry out, "Is there anybody in there?" A baby started to cry loudly. There was more pounding. This whole thing went on for about five minutes. *Where the hell is the instructor? Screw this. I'll get the door.* The motion from my legs trying to push my chair back "woke me up." The instructor suddenly appeared before me, still in the same spot he had been in before. The crying was gone. The pounding was gone. I had "fallen asleep" with my eyes open and "dreamed" the whole thing. Fortunately, I was lucid enough to understand this and went back to taking my exam. By now, I was conditioned to ignore the games my brain was playing, so I never mentioned this episode to anyone.

At the conclusion of the test, the instructor took it from me and began to grade. "OK, let's see, you missed...one, two, three, four, five, six, seven, eight, nine...ten, eleven. You missed eleven total. Congratulations, Sapper." Without smiling or even acknowledging the information, I ambled outside. I put my cap on my head and limped slowly back to my barracks. Though it seemed like a typical day to me at this school, I couldn't help but think, *I finished thirteen miles of a twelve-mile course with the "runs" and no underwear. I took a test on demolitions calculations while listening to an imaginary woman and her baby crying outside the room. What...the...fuck.*

CHAPTER SEVEN

Graduation

"Sapper"

I pulled out my cell phone and sent a mass text to anybody and everybody who knew where I was. Once again, I didn't feel as if I had the right words, but I didn't care. I sent, "OK, I'm a Sapper now." For the rest of that day, I received an enormous number of text messages and several phone calls. I didn't reply to most of them. There was still work to be done for graduation, and I needed a haircut.

It was all over. I guess this is the part where I say, "I wanted to celebrate, so I…" but the reality of it was that I didn't feel much of anything. Again, there was simply nothing to *feel* with. I took a taxi to the PX (post exchange) and limped inside. The pain in my balls and stomach was acute. My hair was long—definitely out of army regulations. Parts of my face were a bit unshaven, and my uniform was tinted green and brown and smelled like cut grass clippings (the laundry detergent couldn't get the stains or the reek out). I looked sallow, my cheeks sunk in a bit, and I looked and felt very weak.

The entrance led directly into the food court, and I took a few seconds to just stand there and take in the scene. There were soldiers and civilians everywhere. Most were eating or ordering. Someone got up and got a refill at a Coke machine next to me. I watched: first the ice, then the soda—all at his command. Someone else threw a sandwich away that was only half-eaten. In a flash, I had this snapshot mental image of Bailey and me sneaking off at night

69

and digging through old trash bags in the field. We found a bag of unopened pretzels and ran off into the woods to split them up and eat them as fast as we could. We came pretty close to being caught, but we were so damn happy to have something to eat. Like Christmas morning happy. My flashback ended. I kept looking around, and there was a group of fresh recruits—probably just graduated basic. They were whooping and hollering and puffing their chests and all that whatnot—and then I lurched forward. I must have made a sorry sight because some folks turned to watch as I hobbled and hauled my beaten body to the counter of a Baskin-Robbins. I never averted my eyes. *Fuck 'em. Piss on them and the fact they take everything in life for granted!* I thought. On several occasions thoughts like this flew through my head, and I would stop myself immediately afterward. *Don't become that. Don't become something you don't want to be—someone different from who you are.* "What would you like to order?" asked the girl behind the counter. "I'll have an Oreo cookie shake," I replied. I gave her the money and sat down. I looked at the thing and took a long sip. The flavor! "Shit," I said under my breath. After a few minutes, I finished the drink. *This is freedom. This Oreo cookie shake is...freedom.*

I cut my hair for graduation, picked up a tab for my uniform, and then headed back. I waved down another taxi and told him where to go. There were a few chemical corps chicks in the back of the cab. They could see I was "injured," and they asked me about it. "It's nothing; what are you guys all about?" I asked, dodging the question. They told me about basic training and the chemical corps and how one of them learned how to drive a Humvee or something. I nodded limply.

"So what about you?" one of the girls asked. I wished they hadn't asked that.

"Uh, I got a little hurt during training is all." It must have come out a bit weird because the conversation flatlined, but I didn't care. I then placed my elbow on the window of the cab and rested my head. The car felt good. The seat felt good. The cleanliness, the dryness, the insect-freeness—it all felt so good...

I woke up to the cabbie saying loudly, "Sir…*sir!*"

"Huh…" I replied groggily.

"We're here, sir. Are you all right?" asked the cabbie. I wiped up the drool on my lip and noticed that some had pooled on my jacket as well. *Whatever.* I had trouble getting out of the car, and the cabbie asked one more time, "Sir, are you OK?" The girls stared at me intently.

I stared at him and then the girls and then came back to my senses somewhat. "Yeah, I…I ummm…" *No words to describe anything at all anymore. All used up. Gone.* I held up my hand and started to twirl my wrist and point at all my surroundings as I got out the door and started walking away from the cab. "I'm uhh…I'm a Sapper," I said, as if I were using that as an excuse for not giving him a straight answer. By the time I uttered the last words, I was almost out of earshot. *Leave me alone. I have an excuse to look and act fucked up…I'm a Sapper and I just finished this damn school.* I was glad to be back at the barracks. Yarborough was yapping about some after-party. Gaylick was watching the rifles and machine guns. The sun was starting to set. This was where I wanted to be right now. If not home, then right here with these guys—with the Sappers.

The next morning, they took Chavez and me to the doctors. During our last mission, the heat had nearly killed poor old Chavez, and I'm not exaggerating, as things turned out.

Meanwhile, this Rastafarian-looking doctor had me drop my pants and then felt up my junk. "Yes…yes, I can feel a lot of swelling, but no burst vessels. Turn your head and cough for me…yes. Good." My stuff was apparently in good health and I was released. I had also developed a strong burning sensation when I peed, and so they checked that too. After determining that I did not have "the drip" (a code word for a sexually transmitted disease), the Rastafarian told me that it was due to acute dehydration. Case closed. On my way back, I thought how funny it was—Sapper school, the school that took so much "balls" to complete, almost cost me my nuts.

Chavez, on the other hand, was so badly broken that he needed to go to the emergency room and be hospitalized. It turned out his kidneys were failing. I hope he made it out of there OK.

Graduation was no big deal. I decided to wear my Ranger Challenge patch during the graduation ceremony. I figured that the army had sent me here, and I was going to get at least one laugh at the expense of the Sapper instructors (especially considering how many laughs they'd had at our expense). Those in the platoon who knew me well enough were ecstatic.

"Voznick," laughed SGT Olson, "you've got some balls of steel if you do that. You might really piss off the instructors."

"Dude, if they were made of steel, I wouldn't be limping. And I don't give a crap what they think anyway," I replied straight-faced. The West Pointers tried to talk me out of it. In fact, they didn't understand the joke at all.

One of them even said to me in a serious and condescending tone, "Look, I know you're probably *really* proud of that patch and you had to do a *whole* lot to earn it, but trust me, leave it off." I could only stare back at him. To me it was a polite way of raising the third digit. I don't care too much for the West Pointers; most of them seem to be off somewhere else at times.

To make a longer story short, I left the patch on there, and that was that. For those who don't understand, this was basically the equivalent of the best man showing up to a wedding in fishing gear carrying a tackle box. This all suited me fine. Many of my buddies appreciated the looks on some of our instructors' faces as I walked up there during the ceremony, "proudly" displaying a patch that is not taken seriously by anyone in the US Army. And yes, almost all the Sapper instructors cussed me out as I snapped clean salutes and shook their hands. CPT Simpson was last in line, and as I shook his hand, he looked at me and, in a hillbilly accent, said, "You're a Ranger!" while nearly crushing my hand in his—but he still tabbed my shoulder. So I got my laugh.

That's my story. In hindsight, I have mixed feelings about the whole thing. It was a school where I learned a lot about myself, and I know I'm better for it. It was a rare opportunity, and certainly I take pride in the six letters that now have a permanent place on the left shoulder of my uniform. I learned how to push myself beyond anything I thought possible. I learned that the guys I trained with here, despite the history or background of some of them, were some of America's best soldiers, top of the line, elite, hands down. I learned from them. Always do your best and take it for granted you mean to do your best. Take care of your people and they'll take care of you.

On the other hand, the school had broken me. I would be lying if I said otherwise, and I'm terrible at lying anyway. Sometimes during the school, I would lay awake at night wondering just how the hell I ended up in there. I was supposed to be racing, camping, playing airsoft, living the good life. That was what I had planned, and instead I was there with little food and almost no sleep—and I had *volunteered* for it. If you think about it like that, it comes off as a pretty rotten deal, as if I should have my head examined or something. During the last day, I experienced a form of delirium, and my body finally failed me. If that school had been a single day longer, I would not have succeeded because, by that point, I had been destroyed.

As I was leaving, at the airport I overheard a woman complaining to a family member on a cell phone. "They won't let me bring two bags on the plane! Isn't that ridiculous?" She continued to make a fuss, and though she was not attracting a crowd, I could hardly restrain myself. Part of me wanted to pick her up by the collar and throw her against the wall. I wanted to scream at her—nothing in particular, just scream words at her that would make her understand that her "problem" that was ruining her day was in fact *nothing*. This woman took it for granted that she had a warm, dry place to sleep at night; that she could go to a fast-food restaurant and eat to her heart's content; that she (probably) had a family or somebody who cared about her; and that there were far worse things in life than not having both your bags with you on the plane. This type of occurrence would become common over the course of the next year or so.

I rolled my eyes and said nothing. I smirked as the line started to move forward to board the plane. *I'm still me. I'm still Ryan Voznick. Nobody and nothing will change that…*

The sun was a few hours away from setting when I finally landed at Ontario, California, airport. I went to the baggage claim, picked up my A-bags, and walked directly outside. Already I could feel people staring at me. My haircut screamed US Army, and the A-bags I was carrying made it look like I was coming back from Iraq, but I insist on never wearing my uniform in public if at all possible. I was wearing torn jeans and a Guns N' Roses T-shirt, and it was probably confusing people. Dad came and picked me up after I sat for about five minutes on the warm, clean, dry pavement of the airport. No ticks, no sweat, no pain, no agony, no yelling, no bombs, no machine guns, no rain, no… *misery.* I still couldn't get over the contrast.

When I got back home, my body and mind took about two weeks to recover. I would eat twice the amount I normally ate. This led to some awkward moments at fast-food joints, where I would order a meal, eat it, then order another, and then order a shake or something on the way out (normally, I can barely finish a single order). My friends would just stare at me while I did this. One time, my parents took me to the local Sizzler, and when a plate of food was brought out to me, I immediately gorged myself as if I had only five minutes to eat as much as I could. I'm sure I made a sorry scene, and it was only after my dad said something about slowing down that I caught myself and realized that I had lost at least a little bit of my civility. I went on a family vacation less than a week after I got back, and in all the pictures taken, I am not smiling. Again, this was another unconscious occurrence because I truly thought I was smiling.

For more than a year after, I had a recurring dream (or nightmare or whatever) that I was back there. I was back there and I knew I shouldn't be there. Sometimes I was a student, other times I was an assistant instructor for some reason, but the feeling was the same: *I shouldn't be here. What am I doing here? No! Not again!* And then I would wake up (sometimes yelling) and realize where I was, and my appreciation for creature comforts, for warmth and safety, for friends and family, was all immediately renewed. Just to set the record straight, this nightmare really was not a problem. It was not a big deal; I just put it in for completeness. If that makes me a coward, a "pussy," or whatever, so be it.

I worried about how I would relate and interact with others. After having the shit kicked out of me for so long, I could foresee a problem. How could I relate to anyone's personal issues from here on out? Certainly there are worse things in life, but I'm talking about the standard bitching, moaning, and complaining—legitimate or not—that we all do on a regular basis. The bar for me was elevated beyond anything the average person would understand. Many times, I would listen to my friends' problems and issues and sit in muted silence, awed at what I once knew was my own interpretation of how bad things could be. These were/are issues that would take time to adjust to. But after some patience and discipline, I feel I've got them pretty well licked.

Back at ROTC, the cadre gave me a feeble congratulations and would say things like, "See, I knew you would be fine, Voznick." My response was to say nothing, and find ways to avoid any interaction to cause this type of comment or conversation. Everyone, especially those in ROTC, would tell me how much of a "badass" I was to have completed this school. Those who told me this did so because of the tab on my shoulder. They know only half of what it means to earn it.

I am a Sapper. I can blow up a bridge, blow down a door. I can fight harder, faster, and better than the majority of my counterparts in the US Army. If my country needs me to, I can jump face-first off a cliff, out of an airplane, or out of a helicopter and into a river. I can march for miles on end and be ready to fight at any instant. This is the half that is well understood by many, and it is true. I can and have done all of these things and more…but to get to this point, there were many unsung discomforts that needed to be endured. Ticks had their way with me. I had to dig through trash to eat. I had to break down mentally and physically. I had to experience all kinds of degradation and discomforts—many things that folks would not care to write down, or most of all, remember as I am trying to do here. This "other half" of being a "badass," it's not the mark of a Hollywood movie hero. There is no half time like there is at a football game. Most certainly, there are no cheerleaders, and, at the end of this movie, the hero does not get the girl. No, the true "badass" throws his pack over his shoulder and goes home, and *he is grateful for just that.*

Epilogue

I hope you enjoyed this account of my experience at the US Army's Sapper Leader Course. Before I wrap up, I have to account for a few loose ends. First, I want to make sure that the reader understands that the bulk of this document, probably 90 percent of it, was written within three months of my return from the school. Therefore, you are not reading a version I wrote years after the fact, but one that is as raw and real as could be. I wrote the balance of this story while it was most fresh in my mind.

In my writing, I refer to the Sapper instructors with disdain and fear. They were the "enemy" in more than one sense and, in a way, that's how I treated them. However, the constant cursing I do on behalf of their actions was more a way of letting off steam. It helped me to endure the training. Never did I utter these thoughts out loud, nor did I have any desire to. The Sapper instructors are some of the best leaders I have ever known. Their knowledge of the craft was superseded only by their abilities as leaders, trainers, and mentors. I have nothing but the highest respect for these men.

Another area I would like to address is the various shows, videos, and other recent media that portray Sapper school. Perhaps the most popular and easiest to find is *Surviving the Cut* by the Discovery Channel. In most of these media, and especially *Surviving the Cut*, the instructors are holding back. I can only attribute the prominent lack of swearing and yelling to the presence of the cameras. *Surviving the Cut* appears to me to be an edited PG version of the school. There is a slightly better video series available on YouTube called *RECON—Military Videos*. This three-part series must have been filmed immediately after the course I attended, as many of the same instructors and some of the students I knew are interviewed. It is a more accurate version of the school because, in my opinion, it does a better job of showing the student-instructor interaction. The instructors would say and do things to the students in order to put additional stress on them, and these videos do a much better job of capturing that aspect.

1LT Darroch, myself, SGT Kettinger
My only picture from Sapper school, taken shortly after graduation
(note my "Ranger Challenge" patch just below the ceremonial Sapper tab)

Made in the USA
Middletown, DE
25 May 2021